MW00576548

Savour

I dedicate this book to my mother and father who made for my brother and me many different kinds of traditional breads and frittata. They were always able to whip up something tasty - even when there wasn't much available in the way of ingredients.

First published in 2006 by New Holland Publishers (NZ) Ltd
Auckland • Sydney • London • Cape Town

www.newhollandpublishers.co.nz

218 Lake Road, Northcote, Auckland, New Zealand
14 Aquatic Drive, Frenchs Forest, NSW 2086, Australia
86–88 Edgware Road, London W2 2EA, United Kingdom
80 McKenzie Street, Cape Town 8001, South Africa

Copyright © 2006 in recipes: Alessandra Zecchini
Copyright © 2006 in photography: Shaun Cato-Symonds
Copyright © 2006 New Holland Publishers (NZ) Ltd

Managing editor: Matt Turner
Project manager: Renée Lang
Food stylist: Alessandra Zecchini
Design: Rachel Kirkland at The Fount

Zecchini, Alessandra.
Savour : irresistible pizzas, pies, tarts and bread / recipes by Alessandra
Zecchini; photographs by Shaun Cato-Symonds.
Includes index.
ISBN-13: 978-1-86966-118-2
ISBN-10: 1-86966-118-4
1. Cookery (Bread) 2. Bread. 3. Pies. 4. Pizza.
I. Cato-Symonds, Shaun. II. Title.
641.815—dc 22

1 3 5 7 9 10 8 6 4 2

Colour reproduction by SC (Sang Choy) International Pte Ltd, Singapore
Printed in China by SNP Leefung

All rights reserved. No part of this publication may be reproduced, stored in a retrieval system, or transmitted in any form or by any means, electronic, mechanical, photocopying, recording or otherwise, without the prior permission of the publishers and copyright holders.

While the author and publishers have made every effort to ensure that the information and instructions in this book are accurate and safe, they cannot accept liability for any resulting injury or loss or damage to property whether direct or consequential.

Savour

Irresistible pizzas, pies, tarts and bread

Alessandra Zecchini

Photography by Shaun Cato-Symonds

NEW HOLLAND

Clockwise from top left: Cherry Tomato Quiche - see page 81; Red Beetroot and Feta Tart - see page 83; Yoghurt Cheese and Dukka Filo Tartlets - see page 101; Tomato Bread - see page 36; Walnut Bread - see page 36; Sourdough - see pages 30-32.

Contents

Basic Focaccia - see page 40

Introduction

There is much more to food than pure nourishment. There is pleasure, tradition, conviviality and, sometimes, discovery. Interestingly, some types of food more than others awaken our senses and our raison d être during the day-to-day habit of eating. To me, these types of food are usually those that we find at the centre of the table, and traditionally shared among the diners, be it sliced or broken.

Bread, so basic yet so important in our society; falls into this category. Then there are pies for winter and quiches for summer, pizza for all the family, frittate and omelettes for when time is an issue. Sadly, much of this food increasingly comes from the freezer compartments in large supermarkets, conveniently packed to fulfil our immediate needs. But does it really? We may not have time to bake our own bread everyday, but to be able to do it just once in a while and feel the satisfaction and smell the tantalising aromas escaping from the oven is a unique experience.

This also applies to other forms of home baking. It's great to be able to say, 'Yes, I made the pastry myself, and the pizza base, too!' And think how impressed your family and friends will be when you present your homemade mozzarella!

Previous generations prepared these things regularly at home without the benefit of inside kitchens, running water and electricity, but now that we are blessed with these aids to modern living, it is so easy to make delicious and nutritious foods at home. So, if you wish to make the most of your kitchen, this book is for you. I truly hope it will prove an inspiring and useful addition to your family recipes and daily life.

Alessandra Zecchini

Margherita with Rocket – see page 15

Make Your Own Pizza

The first pizza (the 'mother' of all pizzas) came from Naples, where strict regulations remain in place to this day to ensure that the 'real Neapolitan pizza' stays unique. These regulations state that the pizza base, which may not contain any kind of fat (not even olive oil), must be put straight onto the pizza oven's floor – unlike most other kinds of pizza that are rolled out and then placed in a pan before baking. The oven has to be built to strict specifications, fuelled only by cherry or olive wood (even when lighting it), and heated to a temperature of 400°C (752°F) in order for it to be hot enough to cook the pizza in less than 2 minutes. The tomato, mozzarella cheese and basil must be specific to the area around Naples so that not only will their individual flavours be true, but also the flavour of the final product.

This chapter is all about making your own pizza and toppings at home – even your own mozzarella cheese – in a way that retains as much as possible the true flavours of an Italian pizza.

Basic Pizza Dough

Here is my recipe for basic dough to make a flat pizza. Note that the only ingredients are flour, yeast, water, and a little salt and sugar. No oil or fat should be used if you want to achieve a traditional 'Neapolitan-style' pizza. This recipe can be doubled without the need to increase the yeast to make a thick slab of pizza. It is so easy to make that all my friends use it regularly, especially those with families to feed!

Ingredients

300ml/10½fl oz warm water
2½ teaspoons active yeast granules
¼ teaspoon sugar
500g/1lb 2oz high-grade flour, plus more
   for dusting
1 large pinch of salt

Makes 6

Put the warm water in a large bowl and add the yeast and sugar. After 5 minutes, when the yeast starts to bubble, add the flour and salt and using your hands work the mixture into a dough for about 10 minutes. You can knead it directly on the table if you like or in the bowl (I prefer to use a bowl because I can carry it around the house with me, check on the children, and still have one hand free to answer the telephone, which always seems to ring when I am kneading!). Shape the dough into a ball, sprinkle with flour and leave it to rise in the bowl covered with a clean teatowel, for about 2 hours.

Punch the dough and knead for 1 minute. Divide into 6 equal parts and roll each to make 6 small balls. Place on a floured surface, dust with flour, then cover with a clean teatowel. Leave them to rise for 30 minutes, then using your hands or a rolling pin flatten them, one at a time, into large circles.

Add the topping of your choice and bake for 2–3 minutes in a wood-fired oven or 7–10 minutes in a conventional oven.

Tips and variations

✳ Don't add too much topping because your pizza can't possibly cook well if it is overloaded. If in doubt, less is best. If you are lucky enough to have a proper wood-fired pizza oven, your flat pizza will cook in 2 minutes (or less). If you have a standard oven, heat it to its maximum temperature and allow 7–10 minutes per pizza. Check underneath to see if it is cooked; it should be lightly golden. However, because each oven is different, you may need a couple of trial runs to get to know how long your oven will take to cook pizza.

Making Your Own Mozzarella Cheese

If I had never lived outside Italy I would probably not have thought of making mozzarella at home. But basic cheese-making is a very useful skill, not really that different from baking bread or preserving fruit, and it provides such satisfaction. While you cannot expect to achieve the quality of a 'real' buffalo mozzarella such as those made in the south of Italy by experts, nevertheless your own mozzarella will probably taste superior to some commercial brands, and of course it will be fresh. You will need a brewer's thermometer and an eye-dropper so you can measure small amounts.

Ingredients

2 litres/68fl oz full cream milk (do not use homogenised)
4 heaped tablespoons natural yoghurt
1ml rennet for junket (see Tips and variations)
1ml cold water
2 pinches of salt

Makes 2–3 medium-sized mozzarella cheeses or many *bocconcini* (cherry-sized mozzarella cheeses)

Pour the milk into a saucepan and remove any clots of cream from the top. (If you have an electric stove use a double boiler for best results.) Gently bring the milk to 38°C (100.4°F), add the yoghurt and stir well. Remove from the heat and cover the pan with a lid. After 10 minutes mix the rennet with the cold water (best measured using a dropper) and add to the milk. Stir for 1 minute, then cover the pan and let it rest for 45 minutes. During this time the temperature should remain constant without further intervention, but if it is a very cold day just turn the heat on for no longer than a few seconds every 15–20 minutes.

Check that the contents of the pan have set, then cut it into 4–5cm (2 inch) squares using a large knife. Leave in the pan and cover for 15 minutes. Cut the squares into walnut-size pieces using a slotted spoon. At this point the small pieces must rest for 3–4 hours, and it is vital that they stay at 35°C (95°F) throughout this time. You can do this by keeping the pan covered and constantly checking the temperature with a thermometer. If necessary, turn the heat on every now and then for a few seconds as described earlier. Check the temperature every so often because if the contents become too hot or too cold they will not acidify enough (Ph level 4.9–5.1) and the mozzarella will not achieve its stretchy texture.

After the contents have rested for 3–4 hours, place a little bit of 'curd' in a cup and cover it with water heated to 90°C (194°F). It's essential to have this temperature correct so you must use your thermometer to check. Stir the curd with a spoon and then lift it out of the water and gently pull it (take care – it will be hot!). If it is ready, it will stretch just like elastic. But if it is not yet at this stage, wait another 15 minutes and try again. Assessing its stretchiness is a knack that you have to learn through experience so don't be discouraged if it takes a while to get the hang of it.

Tip the curd into a small plastic colander (the kind used for draining rice), drain, then transfer it to a bowl. Add the salt, cover completely with water heated to 90°C (194°F) and stir (I use my long, thin 'cheese' thermometer for stirring – its dimensions make it ideal for the job). When the mass starts to form strings tip it into the colander (the one used earlier) and keep stirring. As the hot water drains the mozzarella will form into a big ball. Using your hands, stretch the ball so you can break off pieces to roll into smaller balls.

Small balls – *bocconcini* – are easier to make. Don't roll them too tightly or they will be hard. Place each ball as you form it in a bowl of cold water, making sure it is completely covered with water. Continue until you have used up all the mozzarella mass, then refrigerate overnight. The next day your mozzarella will be ready to eat!

Tips and variations

* Patience is the most important thing in the process of making your own mozzarella. You should also buy some fresh Italian mozzarella to taste before you start making your own so you know what you are aiming to achieve (fresh Italian mozzarella is pure white and soft, not yellow and compact).

* Rennet (also suitable for junket) is available from most supermarkets, while vegetarian rennet can usually be purchased from sympathetic cheese-makers – try one in your area. The rennet purchased from supermarkets tends to be less concentrated than the industrial type, and so if you are using the latter you may need less than 1ml for the amount of milk in my recipe (this is where an eyedropper is very useful). Test to be sure.

Tomato Sauce

Here is how to make the easiest and best tomato sauce ever. As a bonus this sauce can be used with pasta and a variety of other dishes and the quantity can be easily halved or doubled as required.

Ingredients

2 x 400g/14oz cans Italian peeled
  tomatoes
2 cloves garlic, peeled
2 tablespoons olive oil
small handful of fresh basil leaves
salt to taste

Makes enough for 6 or for 1 large thick
  pizza slab

Place the tomatoes including their juice in a blender. Add the garlic and blend until smooth. Rinse out one of the cans with ½ cup water and pour into a large frying pan. Add the blended tomato mixture and bring to the boil. Simmer, stirring from time to time, for at least 30 minutes or until the sauce is so thick that when you stir it with a wooden spoon you can see the bottom of the pan. Add the olive oil, fresh basil leaves and salt to taste. Cover and set aside until needed.

Tips and variations

* Personalise this sauce by adding some tomato paste or a little dried oregano. If you use it with pasta, just add whatever takes your fancy, e.g. capsicums (peppers), mushrooms, parsley, onion, cream and cheese.

Sage and Onion Pizza

Cooking the onions before adding them to pizza will make them taste sweeter.

Ingredients

1 x quantity Basic Pizza Dough
  (see page 10)

TOPPING
3 medium onions
2 tablespoons olive oil
small handful of fresh sage leaves
salt and black pepper to taste
3 large mozzarella cheeses

Makes 6

Make the dough according to the method on page 10 and leave it to rise for about 2 hours.
When the dough has risen, punch and knead for 1 minute, then divide into 6 equal parts. Roll each part into a small ball. Place on a floured surface, dust with flour, cover with a clean teatowel and leave to rise for 30 minutes.
  In the meantime peel and finely slice the onions. Heat the oil in a frying pan and add the onion and sage leaves. Sauté the onion until soft and translucent (take your time doing this – the longer they cook the sweeter they will be). Season to taste and set aside.
  Preheat the oven to 240°C (475°F) or as high as it will go.
  Using either your hands or a floured rolling pin, flatten each ball of pizza dough into a large circle.
  Cut the mozzarella into thick slices and divide between the 6 pizza bases, leaving a 2cm (½ inch) outside border without topping. Cover with the cooked onion and bake for 7–10 minutes, less if your oven can get really hot (or for 2 minutes in a wood-fired oven). Serve immediately.

Tips and variations

* For a dairy-free variation just double the amount of onion and omit the mozzarella. For a more cheesy variation add freshly grated parmesan cheese.

Margherita with Rocket

The classic Margherita is traditionally made with only basil, tomato and mozzarella.

Ingredients

1 x quantity Basic Pizza Dough
(see page 10)
1 x quantity Tomato Sauce (see page 14)

TOPPING
200g/7oz fresh mozzarella cheese
sprinkle of dried oregano (optional)
pinch of salt and drop of olive oil
(optional)
100g/3½oz rocket leaves

Makes 6

Make the dough according to the method on page 10 and leave it to rise for about 2 hours. In the meantime make the tomato sauce.

When the dough has risen, punch and knead for 1 minute, then divide into 6 equal parts. Roll each part into a small ball. Place on a floured surface, dust with flour, cover with a clean teatowel and leave to rise for 30 minutes. Using either your hands or a floured rolling pin, flatten each into a large circle.

Preheat the oven to 240°C (475°F) or as high as it will go.

Spread each circle of dough with the tomato sauce, then top with a few slices of mozzarella and, if you like, a sprinkle of oregano, salt and olive oil.

Bake for 7–10 minutes, less if your oven can get really hot (or for 2 minutes in a wood-fired oven).

Place the rocket leaves on top and serve immediately.

Marinara

Marinara means 'from the sea', yet no seafood can be found on this pizza, just tomato sauce, garlic and herbs.

Ingredients

1 x quantity Basic Pizza Dough
(see page 10)
1 x quantity Tomato Sauce (see page 14)

TOPPING
3 cloves garlic, peeled and finely sliced
3 tablespoons finely chopped Italian
(flat-leaf) parsley
sprinkle of dried oregano (optional)
pinch of salt
drop of olive oil

Makes 6

Make the dough according to the method on page 10 and leave it to rise for about 2 hours. In the meantime make the tomato sauce.

When the dough has risen, punch and knead for 1 minute, then divide into 6 equal parts. Roll each part into a small ball. Place on a floured surface, dust with flour, cover with a clean teatowel and leave to rise for 30 minutes. Using either your hands or a floured rolling pin, flatten each into a large circle.

Preheat the oven to 240°C (475°F) or as high as it will go.

Spread each circle of dough with the tomato sauce, then add the sliced garlic, chopped parsley and, if you like, a sprinkle of oregano. Sprinkle with salt and drizzle with olive oil to taste.

Bake for 7–10 minutes, less if your oven can get really hot (or for 2 minutes in a wood-fired oven).

Serve immediately.

Tips and variations

✱ This makes a great base for a dairy-free pizza, so you can add more toppings if you wish. Thinly sliced capsicums (peppers), or courgettes (zucchini), or olives are just a few ideas. The important thing is, as usual, to keep it simple and don't 'over top'.

Pizza Bianca

I like to add a few rosemary leaves on top for flavour or perhaps a stem of vine-ripened tomatoes for colour.

Ingredients

1 x quantity Basic Pizza Dough
    (see page 10)

TOPPING
3 large mozzarella cheeses
6 generous pinches of salt
6 tablespoons olive oil
fresh rosemary leaves (optional)
vine-ripened tomatoes on the stem
    (optional)
freshly ground black pepper

Makes 6

Make the dough according to the method on page 10 and leave it to rise for about 2 hours.

When the dough has risen, punch and knead for 1 minute, then divide into 6 equal parts. Roll each part into a small ball. Place on a floured surface, dust with flour, cover with a clean teatowel and leave to rise for 30 minutes.

Using either your hands or a floured rolling pin, flatten each into a large circle. Preheat the oven to 240°C (475°F) or as high as it will go.

Cut the mozzarella into thick slices and divide between the bases, leaving a 2cm (½ inch) outside border without topping. Add a generous pinch of salt and 1 tablespoon of olive oil to each pizza and, if you wish, a few rosemary leaves and/or a stem of vine-ripened tomatoes (make sure you puncture the tomatoes with a knife before baking or they may explode in the oven).

Bake for 7–10 minutes, less if your oven can get really hot (or for 2 minutes in a wood-fired oven). Remove from the oven and sprinkle with freshly ground black pepper. Serve immediately.

Tips and variations

✳ The mozzarella should be cut quite thick or it will easily burn in a conventional oven. If your oven takes longer than the 'maximum' 10 minutes to bake the base, add the mozzarella after 5 minutes. Each oven is different and it may take a few trials before working out how to best use yours. In any case, if you bake only one pizza at a time, you can easily test your oven's own 'mozzarella burning point'.

Pizza with Eggplant

Eggplant (aubergine) makes a wonderful topping for pizza, but it does benefit from a period of 'sweating'. In this recipe, the trick is to time the kneading of the dough with the making of the topping.

Ingredients

1 x quantity Basic Pizza Dough
   (see page 10)

TOPPING
4 large tomatoes
1 large eggplant (aubergine)
salt for sprinkling
8 tablespoons olive oil
2 cloves garlic, peeled and finely chopped
pinch of dried oregano
1 large mozzarella cheese
6 generous pinches of salt

Makes 6

Make the dough according to the method on page 10 and leave it to rise for about 2 hours.

In the meantime, dice the tomatoes and eggplant. Drain the tomatoes in a colander. Place the diced eggplant in a bowl, sprinkle with salt and leave to sweat for 1–2 hours.

When the dough has risen, punch and knead for 1 minute, then divide into 6 equal parts. Roll each part into a small ball. Place on a floured surface, dust with flour, cover with a clean teatowel and leave to rise for 30 minutes.

Rinse the diced eggplant and pat dry with a teatowel.

Heat 2 tablespoons of oil in a large frying pan and add the garlic. Add the diced eggplant and sauté for 5 minutes, stirring constantly.

Using your hand, gently press the diced tomato to squeeze out as much water as possible. Add the tomato to the pan with the oregano and stir for 1 minute.

Preheat the oven to 240°C (475°F) or as high as it will go.

Flatten each ball of pizza dough into a large circle using either your hands or a floured rolling pin. Top each base with sauce and bake for 5 minutes, less if your oven can get really hot. Remove from the oven and place 1–2 slices of mozzarella in the centre of each pizza, then add a generous pinch of salt and 1 tablespoon of olive oil. Bake for a further 2 minutes. (If you are using a wood-fired oven top the bases with the mozzarella before baking for 2 minutes.)

Serve immediately.

Tips and variations

✻ This eggplant sauce also works well as a pasta sauce, a pie filler, a tasty antipasto or a sophisticated vegetable side dish. Add a few capers and olives to make a really tasty variation.

Pizza ai 4 Formaggi

Feel free to use whatever combination of cheeses you like on this pizza.

Ingredients

1 x quantity Basic Pizza Dough
  (see page 10)

TOPPING

2 large mozzarella balls, sliced
6 slices gorgonzola cheese
6 slices *scamorza affumicata* or local
  smoked cheese
6 slices firm ricotta cheese

Makes 6

Make the dough according to the method on page 10 and leave it to rise for about 2 hours.

When the dough has risen, punch and knead for 1 minute, then divide into 6 equal parts. Roll each part into a small ball. Place on a floured surface, dust with flour, cover with a clean teatowel and leave to rise for 30 minutes. Using either your hands or a floured rolling pin, flatten each into a large circle.

Preheat the oven to 240°C (475°F) or as high as it will go.

Place the sliced mozzarella over one quarter of each pizza. Divide the rest of the cheese between the 6 pizza bases, keeping them separate so that each quarter has just one kind of cheese. If you have a wood-fired pizza oven, you can bake them immediately. However, if using a conventional oven, bake the bases for 5 minutes in the preheated oven before adding the topping and baking for a further 2–5 minutes.

Serve immediately.

Tips and variations

✱ If you do not have a wood-fired pizza oven, bake the pizza bases separately before adding the cheese topping.

Pizza with Capers and Olives

Large juicy whole olives taste gorgeous on pizza. And capers add a zesty twist.

Ingredients

1 x quantity Basic Pizza Dough
  (see page 10)
1 x quantity Tomato Sauce (see page 14)

TOPPING

200g/7oz fresh mozzarella cheese, sliced
6 tablespoons black or green olives
  (or a combination)
2 teaspoons capers, rinsed and drained
6 pinches of salt
6 tablespoons olive oil

Makes 6

Make the dough according to the method on page 10 and leave it to rise for about 2 hours. In the meantime make the tomato sauce.

When the dough has risen, punch and knead for 1 minute, then divide into 6 equal parts. Roll each part into a small ball. Place on a floured surface, dust with flour, cover with a clean teatowel and leave to rise for 30 minutes. Using either your hands or a floured rolling pin, flatten each into a large circle.

Preheat the oven to 240°C (475°F) or as high as it will go.

Divide the tomato sauce between the six bases. To each add a few slices of mozzarella, then sprinkle over the olives and capers. Sprinkle with salt and drizzle with olive oil to taste.

Bake for 7–10 minutes, less if your oven can get really hot (or for 2 minutes in a wood-fired oven).

Serve immediately.

Pizza ai Pomodorini

This pizza is so easy to make because you don't need to cook the topping.

Ingredients

1 x quantity Basic Pizza Dough
  (see page 10)

TOPPING

1kg/2lb 3oz cherry tomatoes
3 cloves garlic, peeled and sliced
about 20 basil leaves, each torn in half
6 generous pinches of salt
6 tablespoons olive oil

Makes 6

Make the dough according to the method on page 10 and leave it to rise for about 2 hours.
  Cut the cherry tomatoes in half and drain in a colander, shaking them occasionally.
  When the dough has risen, punch and knead for 1 minute, then divide into 6 equal parts. Roll each part into a small ball. Place on a floured surface, dust with flour, cover with a clean teatowel and leave to rise for 30 minutes. Using either your hands or a floured rolling pin, flatten each into a large circle.
  Preheat the oven to 240°C (475°F) or as high as it will go.
  Place the cherry tomatoes in a bowl with the garlic and torn basil leaves. Mix well, then divide between the bases, leaving a 2cm (½ inch) outside border without topping. Sprinkle each with a generous pinch of salt and 1 tablespoon of olive oil and bake for 7–10 minutes, less if your oven can get really hot (or for 2 minutes in a wood-fired oven).
  Serve immediately.

Tips and variations

✳ Substitute fresh basil with dried oregano. If you don't have cherry tomatoes just chop some larger tomatoes into small pieces.

Pizza al Pesto

There is a *pizzeria* in Modena where they make an amazing pizza topped with a thick layer of pesto. One slice is usually enough to satisfy most appetites, so make just one pizza rather than six.

Ingredients

⅙ x quantity Basic Pizza Dough
(see page 10)

TOPPING
3 cups fresh basil leaves
3 cloves garlic, peeled
1 teaspoon toasted pine nuts, plus extra
to decorate
2 tablespoons grated pecorino cheese
2 tablespoons olive oil, plus extra
to drizzle

Makes 1

Prepare the pizza dough according to the instructions on page 10 (remember you are only making enough for 1 pizza).

Preheat the oven to 240°C (475°F) or as high as it will go.

Place the basil leaves, garlic and pine nuts in a large mortar. Using the pestle, work the mixture until it turns into a fine paste (you could use a food processor, but somehow it doesn't taste the same!). Add the grated pecorino and olive oil and work it into the paste for a few minutes.

Bake the base for 5 minutes. Remove from the oven and spread with the pesto. Bake for a further 2 minutes. (If you are using a wood-fired oven top the base with pesto before baking for 2 minutes.) When the pizza is ready, drizzle it with olive oil and decorate with toasted pine nuts. Serve immediately.

Tips and variations

✱ Omit the cheese to make a dairy-free pizza.

Deep Crust Pizza Slab

A slight change to the basic dough for the standard (flat) pizza can make a more hearty meal. It also takes less time and work, and will satisfy many stomachs. In Italy this is called *pizza al trancio* or *pizza al taglio* (cut pizza) and it can be easily made at home.

Ingredients

500ml/17fl oz warm water
3 teaspoons active yeast granules
½ teaspoon sugar
1kg/2lb 3oz high-grade flour, plus extra
    for dusting
large pinch of salt
1 x quantity Tomato Sauce (see page 14)

TOPPING
salt
pinch of dried oregano
olive oil to drizzle
200g/7oz fresh mozzarella cheese, sliced

Makes 1 large 35 x 60cm (14 x 24 inch)
pizza (or 2 smaller ones if you have a
standard-sized oven)

Place the warm water in a large bowl, add the yeast and sugar and set aside for 5 minutes. When the yeast starts to bubble, add the flour and salt. Knead for about 10 minutes (work with it in the bowl or on the table if you prefer). Shape the dough into a ball, place back in the bowl and sprinkle with the extra flour. Leave it to rise, covered with a teatowel, for about 2 hours.

In the meantime make a double batch of tomato sauce according to the instructions on page 14.

Preheat the oven to 230°C (450°F).

Punch the dough and knead it for 1 minute. Press it down with your fingers then stretch it to cover a 35 x 60cm (14 x 24 inch) oven tray lined with baking paper (use 2 standard baking trays if you have a small oven). Top with the tomato sauce, sprinkle with a few generous pinches of salt and a pinch of oregano, and drizzle with olive oil.

Bake for 20–25 minutes. Remove from the oven and add the sliced mozzarella and bake for a further 5–10 minutes.

Serve immediately.

Tips and variations

✳ Add some of your favourite toppings (e.g. olives, artichokes, mushrooms, capsicums, etc) before adding the mozzarella. Just remember the golden rule – don't add too many different toppings or your pizza will become heavy and won't cook properly.

Wholemeal Pizza

This pizza is not traditionally Italian, but as more and more people are turning to wholemeal food for its nutritional value, I have devised a 100% wholemeal dough that is easy to make and tasty, too.

Ingredients

400ml/13fl oz warm water
2½ teaspoons active yeast granules
¼ teaspoon sugar
500g/1lb 2oz wholemeal flour, plus extra
    for dusting
large pinch of salt
2 x quantities Tomato Sauce
    (see page 14)

TOPPING
salt
sprinkle of dried oregano
olive oil to drizzle
300g/10½oz fresh mozzarella cheese

Makes 1 large pizza slab

Place the warm water in a large bowl, add the yeast and sugar and set aside for 5 minutes. When the yeast starts to bubble, add the flour and salt. Knead for about 10 minutes (it will be quite sticky so keep it in the bowl). Shape the dough into a ball and sprinkle generously with the extra flour. Leave it to rise, covered with a teatowel, for about 2 hours.

In the meantime make a double batch of tomato sauce according to the instructions on page 14.

Preheat the oven to 230°C (450°F).

Punch the dough, but don't knead it. Place it directly on an oven tray, lined with baking paper and push it down with your fingers to cover the entire surface of the tray. Top with the tomato sauce, sprinkle with the salt and oregano, and drizzle with olive oil.

Bake for 20–25 minutes. Remove from the oven and add the sliced mozzarella and bake for a further 5–10 minutes.

Serve immediately.

Tips and variations

✴ A wholemeal dough is more filling that an ordinary white dough – and its strong taste also calls for a more substantial topping (the reason for increasing the amount of tomato sauce and mozzarella). Additional toppings can add more flavour, e.g. olives, capsicums (peppers), capers, or a strong cheese such as feta or blue cheese. Add the extra toppings together with the mozzarella so that they will not burn.

Vegetable Calzone

A calzone is really just a folded-over pizza, forming a classical half-moon shape. A calzone will stay hot for longer – so if you are a slow eater and you like your pizza hot, this recipe, which makes a generous number, is for you.

Ingredients

1 x quantity Basic Pizza Dough
   (see page 10)

FILLING

1kg/2lb 3oz courgettes (zucchini)
   or see Tips and variations for other
   vegetable fillings
3 tablespoons olive oil, plus extra for
   brushing
2 cloves garlic, finely chopped
½ teaspoon salt
3 tablespoons finely chopped Italian
   (flat-leaf) parsley
freshly ground black pepper (optional)
pinch of dried oregano (optional)

Makes 6

Make the dough according to the method on page 10 and leave to rise for about 2 hours.

In the meantime wash the courgettes and slice finely. In a heavy-bottomed pan heat the oil with the garlic. As soon as the garlic starts to sizzle add the sliced courgette and stir for 1–2 minutes until coated with oil. Add the salt, cover, and simmer for about 15 minutes, stirring from time to time. Uncover and simmer further until all the water has evaporated (the courgettes need to become quite dry or the calzone will turn soggy). Remove from heat, add the parsley and black pepper and/or oregano if desired. Set aside to cool completely.

When the dough has risen, punch and knead for 1 minute, then divide into 6 equal parts. Roll each part into a small ball. Place on a floured surface, dust with flour, cover with a clean teatowel and leave to rise for 30 minutes.

Using either your hands or a floured rolling pin, flatten each into a large circle. Preheat the oven to 240°C (475°F) or as high as it will go.

Spread some cooked courgette mixture over half of each calzone, leaving an outside border of about 2cm (½ inch). Fold the uncovered half over to enclose the filling and pinch the edges to seal them well.

Bake for 7–10 minutes, less if your oven can get really hot (or for 2 minutes in a wood-fired oven).

Remove from the oven, brush with the extra olive oil and serve immediately.

Tips and variations

* Calzone offer endless variations. In fact, you can make a calzone with anything you like. Some of my favourite fillings include red cabbage; combinations of mozzarella, tomatoes and oregano; roast capsicums (peppers); or spinach and feta.
* Various types of cabbage are also suitable for this recipe, but I like the bright colour of red cabbage. Add some cheese (mozzarella works well) if you like.
* Red cabbage, simply cooked with a little vegetable stock, makes a good vegetable side dish, a healthy pasta sauce, or the base for a purple risotto.
* This Italian treat can be frozen and used, one or two at a time, at a later date.

Calzone ai Funghi

Funghi is the Italian word for mushrooms, which make a rich filling and a great-tasting calzone.

Ingredients

1 x quantity Basic Pizza Dough
  (see page 10)

FILLING
50g/2oz dried porcini mushrooms
1kg/2lb 3oz fresh mushrooms (any type)
2 cloves garlic, peeled and finely chopped
1 small carrot, scrubbed and finely
  chopped
1 stalk celery, finely chopped
2 tablespoons olive oil, plus extra for
  brushing
1 x 400g/14oz can Italian tomatoes
salt and pepper to taste
2 tablespoons finely chopped Italian
  (flat-leaf) parsley

Makes 6

Make the dough according to the method on page 10 and leave to rise for about 2 hours.

In the meantime soak the porcini in a little warm water for 30 minutes. Clean the fresh mushrooms and cut any large ones in half. Place the chopped garlic, carrot and celery in a large saucepan with the olive oil and sauté for 2 minutes. Add the fresh mushrooms and sauté for a further 2 minutes. Stir in the porcini mushrooms and their water, the can of tomatoes including the juice and a little salt and pepper. Simmer for approximately 40 minutes over low heat, stirring occasionally, until the sauce has become quite thick. Check seasoning and adjust if necessary. Add the chopped parsley, then set aside to cool.

When the dough has risen, punch and knead for 1 minute, then divide into 6 equal parts. Roll each part into a small ball. Place on a floured surface, dust with flour, cover with a clean teatowel and leave to rise for 30 minutes.

Using either your hands or a floured rolling pin, flatten each into a large circle. Preheat the oven to 240°C (475°F) or as high as it will go.

Spread some mushroom mixture over half of each calzone, leaving an outside border of about 2cm. Fold the uncovered half over to enclose the filling and pinch the edges to seal well.

Bake for 7–10 minutes, less if your oven can get really hot (or for 2 minutes in a wood-fired oven). Remove from the oven, brush with olive oil and serve immediately.

Tips and variations

✱ I like to use a variety of different mushrooms, including wild ones when I can find them, but as these are not always available, button mushrooms make a suitable substitute as long as their flavour is intensified by the addition of dried porcini. This filling mixture is great for other kinds of pies as well as for a pasta sauce.

Easy Bread - see page 53

Bread & Focaccia

Homemade bread has an irresistible appeal. Everything that goes into it – the hand-kneading, the fragrance, the taste – contributes to a truly satisfying experience. My own preference is for the simplest and most ancient kind of dough, a combination of flour and water, so I have included a couple of sourdough recipes that make use of the natural yeasts present in the air. Then there are a number of easy yeast loaves: from *ciabatta* to rye bread, from *naan* bread to some olive-oil rich *focacce*, as well as some fancy doughs for special occasions. They are all aimed at inspiring the first-time bread-maker as well as the more experienced. I do hope your kitchen will soon fill with the beautiful fragrance of a freshly baked loaf.

Sourdough from the Beginning

In Europe many rural families still make their own sourdough, usually once a week. But getting the recipe for a sourdough starter is not easy because most people use dough from the previous batch as a starter – a practice they've been following for many years. It takes a few days to make a sourdough from the beginning, so it pays to plan ahead, e.g. if you want your loaf for Sunday lunch, you will need to start on Wednesday morning.

Ingredients

STEP 1
200g/7oz wholemeal flour
300ml/10fl oz warm water

STEP 2
100ml/3½fl oz warm water
200g/7oz high-grade flour

STEP 3
50ml/2fl oz warm water
250g/9oz high-grade flour, plus extra
  for dusting
generous pinch of salt

Makes 1 loaf

Four full days before you want to serve the bread, mix together the wholemeal flour and the first measure of water in a large mixing bowl using your fingers. The dough will look very sticky, but this is normal. Cover the bowl with a damp teatowel and let it rest for 2 days. If the air is very dry, keep the teatowel good and damp. The principle of sourdough is to make use of the natural yeasts present in the atmosphere, so it's best not to leave the dough in a cupboard.

As early as possible on the third day, add the second measure of warm water and mix it through with your fingers. Still using your fingers, add the high-grade flour and mix it well. Cover the bowl with a damp teatowel and set aside again, this time for at least 24 hours.

Add the third measure of warm water and mix it through, followed by the second measure of high-grade flour and the salt. Knead well in the bowl until the dough is no longer sticky. Dust the mass with flour and cover with a damp teatowel.

Approximately 12 hours later, punch the dough and knead again briefly. (If you want some starter dough for future bread-making occasions, this is the time to pull off a small piece of dough (170–200g/6–7oz) from the mass and put it aside in a small bowl covered with a damp teatowel. It will keep for 2–3 days, longer in winter. See page 32 for further instructions.) Shape the remaining dough into a neat ball, dust well with flour and place on a baking tray lined with baking paper. Cover with a large bowl, slightly tilted to leave a little opening at the bottom to air the dough and leave it to rise overnight.

The next day, take a sharp knife and make a few light incisions on the top of your loaf. Bake in a preheated 220°C (425°F) oven for 30 minutes or until the loaf is well cooked, the crust is quite dark, and it sounds hollow when you tap it on the bottom.

Allow the loaf to cool before slicing. Note: This loaf keeps well for up to 1 week.

Tips and variations

✳ Don't be frightened by the amount of time involved. There's not actually that much to do, apart from a bit of kneading now and then, because natural yeasts present in the air will do the rest. And nothing drastic will happen if you work on it one or two hours earlier or later: it will still taste good. When you make it for the first time, the loaf will be quite flat; but subsequent doughs will be firmer, so don't worry too much about aesthetics at this stage. (I am sure that my great-grandmother, with children to look after, never-ending housework plus her field work, didn't ever worry about making two loaves the same!) To find out what to do with the small piece of reserved starter dough, see recipe on page 32.

Consecutive Sourdough Loaves

When you have made your own sourdough starter, treat it as a family treasure. It will keep well for a couple of days at room temperature (up to 3 days in winter or in the fridge), stored in a small bowl and covered with a damp teatowel.

Ingredients

STEP 1
170–200g/6–7 oz starter dough
   (see page 30)
200ml/7fl oz warm water
200g/7 oz high-grade flour

STEP 2
50ml/2fl oz warm water
250g/9oz high-grade flour, plus extra
   for dusting
generous pinch of salt

Makes 1 loaf

Place the starter dough in a large bowl, add the first measure of warm water and mix with your fingers until it feels squishy. Add the first measure of flour and mix well for a few minutes. Cover the bowl with a damp teatowel and set it aside in a quiet corner to rest.

About 30–36 hours later, add the second measure of warm water and mix it in. Add the second measure of flour and the salt. Knead well in the bowl until the dough is no longer sticky. Dust with flour, cover with the damp teatowel and set aside again, this time for about 8–12 hours.

Punch the dough and knead again briefly. At this stage, pull off a small piece of dough (170–200g/6–7oz) and put it aside in a small bowl covered with a damp teatowel as your starter for future bread. Shape the remaining dough into a neat ball, dust well with flour and place on a baking tray lined with baking paper. Cover with a large bowl, slightly tilted to leave a little opening at the bottom to air the dough, and leave it to rise for about 8 hours.

Bake in a preheated 220°C (425°F) oven for 30 minutes or until the loaf is well cooked, the crust is quite dark and it sounds hollow when you tap it on the bottom

Allow the loaf to cool before slicing. Note: This loaf keeps well for up to 1 week.

Tips and variations

✳ As stated earlier, don't panic if you work on the dough earlier or later than the recommended times. The only thing to worry about is not burning the bread during baking!

✳ Consecutive loaves will be easier to make, and they will also be whiter in colour. By all means have some fun by occasionally adding different kinds of flours, but remember that wholemeal, spelt and rye flours will require a little more water than high-grade and strong flours.

✳ If at some point in the future you cannot bake for any reason, why not make the dough anyway, then keep a little starter for yourself, and present the rest to a friend. Or, if you are going away, you could give your starter to your neighbour, complete with instructions, and collect a fresh piece of starter on your return. It's also possible to freeze the starter.

Easy Bread

Italian-style homemade bread is often quite hard in texture, making it the best type to slice and for mopping up sauces. As this recipe makes two loaves, I always make them slightly different to add interest.

Ingredients

500ml/17fl oz warm water
2½ teaspoons active yeast granules
¼ teaspoon sugar
1kg/2lb 3oz high-grade flour, plus extra
   for dusting
½ teaspoon salt
olive oil for brushing
rock salt

Makes 2 loaves

Place half the warm water in a large bowl, add the yeast and sugar, then set aside for 5 minutes. When the yeast starts to bubble, add the flour, salt and the rest of the water and work into a dough for about 10 minutes. When the dough stops sticking to your fingers, you can knead it directly on the table. Shape the dough into a ball, sprinkle with flour and leave to rise in the bowl, covered with a teatowel, for about 2 hours.

Punch the dough and knead it for 1 minute, then divide into 2 pieces. Using both hands, one for each, knead the dough for a further 2 minutes. Shape each loaf as you please (e.g. round or slightly elongated). Sprinkle one generously with flour, then make several diagonal incisions on top with a knife. Brush the other loaf with the olive oil, again making several incisions, this time diamond-shaped (or similar), then sprinkle with the rock salt. Place the loaves on a baking tray lined with baking paper and leave to rise for 30 minutes. Bake in a preheated 250°C (500°F) oven for 30 minutes or until well cooked, the crusts are dark, and they sound hollow when tapped on the bottom.

Tips and variations

✳ Store the bread in a plastic bag to keep it fresh. When it becomes too hard to enjoy, use it to make bruschetta.

Spelt Bread

Spelt is a type of wheat that produces a fragrant, soft bread with a distinctive flavour. It almost disappeared last century in favour of 'proper' wheat, but its highly digestible qualities have resulted in a comeback.

Ingredients

400ml/13fl oz warm water
2½ teaspoons active yeast granules
¼ teaspoon sugar
500g/1lb 2oz spelt flour
generous pinch of salt

Makes 1 loaf

Place the warm water in a large bowl, add the yeast and sugar, then set aside for 5 minutes. When the yeast starts to bubble, add the spelt flour and salt and mix for 5 minutes, using just one hand. This dough will be very sticky and should come off the sides of the bowl in a big lump. Pick it up in 1 whole piece and place in a very well-greased 23 x 13cm (9 x 5 inch) loaf tin. Cover with a damp teatowel and leave it to rise for about 30 minutes.

Bake in a preheated 200°C (400°F) oven for 35–40 minutes or until well cooked and the loaf comes out of the tin easily.

Tips and variations

✳ Spelt flour can be found in health food and organic shops. There is also a wholemeal variety, which can be used for the same recipe, but you will need to add a little more water.

Wholemeal Bread

This is my own recipe for an easy wholemeal bread, which is not only suitable for beginners, but will be also appreciated by more experienced bread-makers for its clean and uncomplicated taste. Light yet satisfying, it will last well for a few days, its flavour improving as time goes on.

Ingredients

500ml/17fl oz warm water
2 teaspoons active yeast granules
1 teaspoon brown sugar
500g/1lb 2oz wholemeal flour, plus extra
   for dusting
½ teaspoon salt

Makes 1 large loaf

Place half the warm water in a large bowl, add the yeast and sugar, then set aside for 5 minutes. When the yeast starts to bubble, add the flour, salt and the rest of the water and work into a dough for about 5 minutes using your fingers. This dough will be too sticky to roll on the table so it must be kneaded in the bowl.

Line a baking tray with baking paper and sprinkle generously with flour. Turn out the dough on the tray, without spreading it too much, and sprinkle with flour, especially over the edges. Use a very large bowl to cover the dough. Alternatively sprinkle more flour over and cover with a teatowel. Leave the dough to rise for about 2 hours. When the time is up, move it around by lifting and shaking the edges of the baking paper for a few minutes in such a way that it turns over and takes on a more 'bread-like' shape. Add more flour if the sides are too sticky. Leave to rise for 30 minutes, then bake in a preheated 250°C (500°F) oven for approximately 30 minutes or until the loaf is well cooked and makes a hollow noise when tapped on the bottom.

Tips and variations

✳ The crust will be quite crunchy to begin with, but as it cools down it will soften. To achieve a consistent crust texture, turn the loaf over a couple of times during the cooling-down period. This simple but tasty bread is great spread with butter or enjoyed with some good cheese.

Rye Bread

Slices of rye bread taste fantastic with sweet or savoury spreads and toppings. I particularly like it with some strong-tasting cheese, or honey, or just plain butter.

Ingredients

300ml/10fl oz warm water
2 teaspoons active yeast granules
½ teaspoon brown sugar
300g/10½oz rye flour, plus extra
    for dusting
200g/7oz high-grade flour
1 teaspoon salt
1 tablespoon molasses
1 teaspoon caraway seeds

Makes 1 loaf

Place the warm water in a large bowl, add the yeast and brown sugar, then set aside for 5 minutes. When the yeast starts to bubble, add both kinds of flour, salt, molasses and caraway seeds. Work into a dough for about 10 minutes using your fingers; it will be quite sticky so knead it in the bowl. Shape into a ball, sprinkle it with rye flour and leave to rise in the bowl, covered with a damp teatowel, for about 2 hours.

Punch the dough and knead it for 1 minute. Form into an oval shape, sprinkle with more rye flour and place on a baking tray lined with baking paper. Leave the dough to rise for 1½ hours.

Bake in a preheated 230°C (450°F) oven for approximately 30 minutes or until the loaf makes a hollow sound when tapped on the bottom.

Tips and variations

✳ Although the crust on this bread looks very dark, don't worry – the bread is not burnt! Rye bread will last for up to 3–4 days and also freezes well. For a change, try using fennel or parsley seeds instead of caraway seeds.

Tomato Bread

Based on one of the most famous Italian staples, tomato paste, this recipe makes a delicious and colourful bread. The sun-dried tomatoes add interest and texture.

Ingredients

500ml/17fl oz warm water
2½ teaspoons active yeast granules
¼ teaspoon sugar
800g/1lb 12oz high-grade flour
½ teaspoon salt
1 teaspoon tomato paste
8–10 sun-dried tomatoes in oil,
   roughly chopped

Makes 1 large loaf

Place half the warm water in a large bowl, add the yeast and sugar, then set aside for 5 minutes. When the yeast starts to bubble, add the flour, salt, tomato paste, the rest of the water and the sun-dried tomatoes including oil. Work into a dough for about 5 minutes using your fingers; it will be quite sticky so knead it in the bowl. Shape the dough into a ball and leave it to rise in the bowl, covered with a damp teatowel, for about 2 hours.

Punch the dough and knead it for 1 minute. Form into a ball again and place on a baking tray lined with baking paper. Leave to rise for 30 minutes, then adjust the shape with your hands (e.g. pull the top up to form a little crown or roll it into a rugby ball shape). Bake in a preheated 220°C (425°F) oven for 30 minutes or until the loaf is well cooked and makes a hollow sound when tapped on the bottom.

Tips and variations

✳ For a more intense flavour, add a pinch of dried oregano or a little paprika.

Walnut Bread

This highly nutritious dark loaf has a distinctive taste and aroma, and goes well with jam, honey, or strong cheeses such as gorgonzola and Stilton.

Ingredients

300ml/10fl oz warm water
2½ teaspoons active yeast granules
¼ teaspoon sugar
400g/14oz high-grade flour, plus extra
   for dusting
100g/3½oz walnut flour (available from
   health food shops)
generous pinch of salt

Makes 1 loaf

Place the warm water in a large bowl, add the yeast and sugar, then set aside for 5 minutes. When the yeast starts to bubble, add both kinds of flour and the salt and work into a dough for about 10 minutes using your fingers. Shape the dough into a ball, sprinkle with the extra flour and leave it to rise in the bowl, covered with a damp teatowel, for about 2 hours.

Punch the dough and knead it for 1 minute, then shape into a long loaf. Place on a baking tray lined with baking paper. Sprinkle the top with a little high-grade flour, and leave it to rise for 30 minutes.

Take a large knife and make a few oblique incisions on the top. Bake in a preheated 220°C (425°F) oven for 30 minutes or until the loaf makes a hollow sound when tapped on the bottom.

Tips and variations

✳ As this bread is quite filling, it's best cut thinly. Add a few walnut pieces to the dough. For a lighter taste use 450g (1lb) of high-grade flour and 50g (2oz) of walnut flour.

Balsamic Onion Bread

A yummy flat loaf filled with onions cooked in balsamic vinegar. Here it is important to know what kind of balsamic vinegar you are using. The real Aceto Balsamico di Modena is DOC (i.e name controlled) and aged at least 12 years. An 8-year-old vinegar is also suitable as it is already sweet enough for this recipe. Anything more acidic than this and you will need to add a little sugar to your onions.

Ingredients

FOR THE DOUGH
250ml/8½fl oz warm water
2½ teaspoons active yeast granules
¼ teaspoon sugar
500g/1lb 2oz high-grade flour, plus extra
    for dusting
pinch of salt, plus extra for sprinkling

FILLING
1 medium red onion
20g/¾oz butter
pinch of salt
1 teaspoon Aceto Balsamico di Modena
1 teaspoon sugar (to add if you are not
    using real Aceto Balsamico)

Makes 1 loaf

Place the warm water in a large bowl, add the yeast and sugar, then set aside for 5 minutes. When the yeast starts to bubble, add the flour and salt and start kneading. This dough is a little dry, so you will need to work patiently to make it nice and elastic; you will know when it is ready. Shape the dough into a ball and sprinkle with flour. Using a sharp knife, cut a cross-shaped incision on the top. Leave it to rise in the bowl, covered with a damp teatowel, for about 2 hours.

In the meantime peel and finely chop the onion. Add the butter to a pan and sauté the onion with a pinch of salt, stirring constantly, until well coloured. Add the balsamic vinegar and stir well. (If the vinegar is a bit too acidic, add the sugar at this point and stir it through so it melts completely.) Remove from the heat and allow to cool.

Punch the dough and knead it for 1 minute. Flatten into a large oval shape, then spread the cooked onion over half the dough. Fold the other half over to cover and seal by pinching the edges together. Place on a baking tray lined with baking paper. Leave the loaf to rise for 30 minutes, then sprinkle with the salt.

Bake in a preheated 250°C (500°F) oven with a pan of water placed on the oven floor (to produce some steam) for about 25 minutes. If after 15 minutes it looks too brown on top, turn the loaf upside down. Remove from the oven and allow to cool for a few minutes before wrapping it, while still warm, in a teatowel and placing it inside a plastic bag. It will soften further as it cools down.

Tips and variations

* You can serve this bread straight from the oven while the crust is deliciously crunchy. For a sweeter taste, add a few sultanas to the onion mixture.

Ciabatta

If you like a soft and chewy ciabatta follow this recipe and store any leftover bread in a sealed plastic bag.
If you prefer a ciabatta with a crunchy crust, eat it while it's still warm – yum!

Ingredients

300ml/10fl oz warm water
2 teaspoons active yeast granules
¼ teaspoon sugar
300g/10½oz high-grade flour, plus extra
    for dusting
pinch of salt

Makes 1 loaf

Place the warm water in a large bowl, add the yeast and sugar and set aside for
5 minutes. When the yeast starts to bubble, add the flour and salt and work into a
dough for about 5 minutes using your fingers. This dough will be too sticky to roll on
the bench or table so knead it in the bowl (although it feels more like mixing). Cover
the bowl with a damp teatowel and leave to rise for about 2 hours.

Line a large baking tray with baking paper and turn out the risen dough onto the tray
bottom-side up. The dough will be sticky so you will need to scrape it from the sides of
the bowl; it is also likely to be runny – prop up the outside edges of the baking paper
with a couple of small ovenproof ramekins to avoid ending up with an extremely large
flat loaf (the ramekins can be filled with water to create a steam oven effect). Dust the
top of the loaf with the extra flour.

Bake in a preheated 180°C (350°F) oven for 25–30 minutes.

Remove the bread from the oven, wrap in a teatowel, then place in a plastic bag and
seal. Leave the bread in the bag for 30 minutes so that the steam will cook it further
and make it soft and deliciously chewy.

Tips and variations

✱ Although some recipes add 1–2 tablespoons of olive oil to the dough, I prefer an oil-
free version so I can drizzle olive oil on it when it is freshly cut and ready to eat. I also
like to dip ciabatta slices in a little oil flavoured with crushed cumin seeds and salt or
basil leaves.

Basic Focaccia

This is my basic focaccia, also known as 'poor focaccia', because in Italy it's made with *salamoia*, a mixture of water, salt and olive oil (thus making the precious and expensive olive oil go further).

Ingredients

600ml/20fl oz warm water
3 teaspoons active yeast granules
¼ teaspoon sugar
1kg/2lb 3oz high-grade flour, plus extra
    for dusting
generous pinch of salt
rock salt (optional)

SALAMOIA
1 teaspoon salt
50ml/2fl oz hot water
25ml/1fl oz olive oil

Makes 1 large 35 x 60cm (14 x 24 inch)
focaccia loaf (or 2 smaller ones)

Place a little of the warm water in a large bowl, add the yeast and sugar, then set aside for 5 minutes. When the yeast starts to bubble, add the flour, salt and the rest of the water and work into a dough for about 10 minutes using your fingers. When the dough no longer sticks to your fingers you can knead it directly on the table or bench. Shape the dough into a ball and dust with a little flour. Place back in the bowl and leave it to rise, covered with a damp teatowel, for about 2 hours.

Punch the dough and knead it for 1 minute. Press down on it with your fingers and stretch it to cover a 35 x 60cm (14 x 24 inch) baking tray lined with baking paper. If you have a small oven, stretch it over 2 baking trays. Leave the dough to rise for 30 minutes.

Preheat the oven to 230°C (450°F).

Prepare the *salamoia* by placing the salt in a bowl and adding the hot water. When the salt has dissolved, add the oil and stir.

Using your fingers, make lots of indentations on the dough, then brush a little *salamoia* over the top. Sprinkle with rock salt if desired.

Bake for 20 minutes, then brush with the remainder of the *salamoia*. Return the bread to the oven and bake for a further 5–10 minutes until golden. Serve hot or cold.

Tips and variations

✳ For a herbed focaccia, sprinkle over some fresh rosemary or thyme leaves before returning the bread to the oven for the last 5–10 minutes (any earlier and the herbs will burn). Or mix some finely chopped Italian (flat-leaf) parsley with 2 chopped garlic cloves and a little salt. Add this mixture to the remaining *salamoia* and spread it over the top of the loaf before returning it to the oven for the last 5–10 minutes.

Focaccia with Potatoes

From a nutritionist's perspective, loading carbohydrate upon carbohydrate may seem strange, but this tasty focaccia is quite popular in Italy. If you are worried about your waistline, have a small slice.

Ingredients

300ml/10fl oz warm water
2½ teaspoons active yeast granules
¼ teaspoon sugar
50ml/2fl oz olive oil, plus extra for
　brushing
600g/1lb 5oz high-grade flour, plus extra
　for dusting
generous pinch of salt, plus extra for
　sprinkling
2–3 large potatoes

Makes 1 large focaccia

Make the dough according to the instructions for Focaccia with Olives on page 43. Using a rolling pin, roll it out to cover a 38 x 28cm (15 x 11 inch) baking tray lined with baking paper. Brush the dough with a little olive oil and leave it to rise for 30 minutes.

Preheat the oven to 250°C (500°F).

Wash the potatoes (peeling is optional) and cut them into very thin round slices. Place the potato slices over the loaf in a regular pattern so that they cover the entire surface but do not overlap. Brush with some more oil and sprinkle with salt. Bake for 25–30 minutes or until the loaf is golden, top and bottom, and the potatoes are cooked.

Tips and variations

✳ Eat hot or cold. Brush the loaf with basil pesto before topping with the potato slices. Add thin slivers of garlic and fresh rosemary leaves, or cheese (such as mozzarella, or your favourite blue cheese, or edam, etc) for the last 5 minutes in the oven (any earlier and it will burn). Top the cooked loaf with fresh rocket leaves or sprinkle with truffle oil. If the potato slices cook before the loaf itself is ready, cover the top with a sheet of aluminium foil and continue baking.

Focaccia di Polenta

Here is a great bread alternative for those who are trying to stay away from wheat and yeast products. As a bonus, this dish is easy to prepare and does not require kneading.

Ingredients

500g/1lb 2oz polenta
olive oil for brushing
rock salt for sprinkling
1 sprig fresh rosemary

Makes 1 large focaccia

Make the polenta according to the instructions on the packet (don't forget to salt the water). As soon as the polenta is ready, pour it onto a 38 x 28cm (15 x 11 inch) baking tray, lined with baking paper, or use two smaller trays. Using a spatula, spread the polenta out to create a large 2cm-thick (just under 1 inch) focaccia shape. Allow to cool completely, ideally overnight, before brushing the surface with olive oil and sprinkling it with rock salt.

Bake in a preheated 180°C (350°F) oven for 15 minutes. Remove from the oven and sprinkle with the rosemary leaves, then bake for a further 10–15 minutes. Allow the loaf to cool slightly, then slice and enjoy.

Tips and variations

✳ Top with different herbs, or finely sliced garlic or some melting cheese (but as it melts very quickly be sure to add it for only the last minute or two of baking).

Filoni e Panini

This is a light wholemeal bread recipe that is suitable for bread sticks (*filoni*) and bread rolls (*panini*). It's easy to make and suitable for an attractive bread basket for the meal table.

Ingredients

600ml/20fl oz warm water
3 teaspoons active yeast granules
¼ teaspoon sugar
200g/7oz wholemeal flour, plus extra
   for dusting
600g/1lb 5oz high-grade flour
½ teaspoon salt

Makes 2 breadsticks or 16 panini

Place half the warm water in a large bowl, add the yeast and sugar, then set aside for 5 minutes. When the yeast starts to bubble, add both types of flour, the salt and the rest of the water. Work into a dough for about 10 minutes using your fingers. When the dough no longer sticks to your fingers, shape it into a ball and sprinkle with wholemeal flour. Leave it to rise in the bowl, covered with a damp teatowel, for about 2 hours.

Punch the dough and knead it for 1 minute. Using a sharp knife, cut it in half and knead both parts for 2 more minutes (use both hands at the same time, i.e. one hand per dough ball). For bread sticks, shape each piece of dough into a long stick, sprinkle with flour and place on a baking tray lined with baking paper. Leave to rise for 30 minutes, covered with a damp teatowel. For bread rolls, cut each of the 2 pieces of dough into 8 small balls (16 altogether) and shape as you please. Sprinkle with flour and leave them to rise on the baking tray for 30 minutes.

Just before baking, take a sharp knife and cut several oblique lines on top of each bread stick or cut a cross shape on each roll.

Bake in a preheated 220°C (425°F) oven for 35–40 minutes for the bread sticks, and approximately 20 minutes for the bread rolls. The bread will be cooked when it makes a hollow sound when tapped on the bottom.

Tips and variations

✳ Make 1 bread stick and 8 rolls, each shaped differently, to add interest and variety. Sprinkle rolls with extra flour or seeds of your choice before baking. Brush rolls with olive oil or rub with butter as soon as they are baked.

Focaccia with Olives

You can use green or black olives or even stuffed olives in this focaccia recipe.

Ingredients

400ml/13fl oz warm water
2½ teaspoons active yeast granules
¼ teaspoon sugar
50ml/2fl oz olive oil, plus extra for
 brushing
600g/1lb high-grade flour, plus extra
 for dusting
generous pinch of salt, plus extra
 for sprinkling
40 olives

Makes 1 large focaccia loaf

Place the warm water in a large bowl, add the yeast and sugar, then set aside for 5 minutes. When the yeast starts to bubble, add the olive oil, flour and salt and work into a dough for about 10 minutes using your fingers. When the dough no longer sticks to your fingers you can knead it directly on the table. Shape into a ball, brush with a little olive oil and leave it to rise in the bowl, covered with a damp teatowel, for about 2 hours.

Punch the dough and knead it for 1 minute. Press it down with your fingers and using a rolling pin roll it out to cover a 38 x 28cm (15 x 11 inch) baking tray lined with baking paper. Brush with a little more olive oil and leave it to rise for 30 minutes.

Preheat the oven to 250°C (500°F).

Place the olives in 8 rows of 5 on top in a regular pattern, pushing them down lightly with your fingers so they stay in position. Sprinkle with a little salt and bake for 25–30 minutes or until the focaccia is golden, top and bottom.

Tips and variations

* Eat hot or cold. Use green and black olives in alternating rows for an interesting effect. Make it without olives – it's just as good plain!

Focaccine Soffici

The Italian word *focaccina* means 'small focaccia', and *soffice* means soft. These bread rolls can be cut and used the same as panini (i.e. with your favourite filling), or sliced and used with dips or to mop up sauces.

Ingredients

300ml/10fl oz warm water
2½ teaspoons active yeast granules
¼ teaspoon sugar
500g/1lb 2oz high-grade flour, plus extra
    for dusting
generous pinch of salt, plus extra
    for sprinkling
olive oil for brushing

Makes 6

Place the warm water in a large bowl, add the yeast and sugar, then set aside for 5 minutes. When the yeast starts to bubble, add the flour and salt and work into a dough for about 10 minutes using your fingers. Shape into a ball, sprinkle with flour and leave it to rise in the bowl, covered with a damp teatowel, for about 2 hours.

Punch the dough and knead it for 1 minute. Divide into 6 equal parts and roll into 6 small balls. Using your hands, shape each ball into a flat disc about 12cm (4½ inches) in diameter. Place them on a baking tray lined with baking paper. Brush with olive oil and leave them to rise for 30 minutes.

Preheat the oven to 200°C (400°F) and place a baking pan full of water on the bottom of the oven to create some steam. Sprinkle the rolls with salt and bake on the top tray for 15 minutes or until they have just changed colour (if you prefer a crunchy crust, bake the rolls for 5 more minutes). Allow to cool slightly before serving.

Tips and variations

✳ Sprinkle the top with dried herbs and/or seeds such as sage, oregano, or cumin.

Gnocco Fritto

Gnocco Fritto, a kind of fried bread, is a specialty of Emilia Romagna, the region in Italy where my family lives. It differs greatly from place to place, not just because of the variation in ingredients, but because of the quality of the water. I think the best one is made in the villages high in the mountains, where the water is purest. It is for this reason that many plain dwellers use mineral water, rather than tap water.

Ingredients

1 x quantity Easy Bread
  (see page 33) or 1 x quantity Basic Pizza
  Dough (see page 10)
good quality vegetable oil for frying
salt (optional)

Makes lots

Make the bread dough according to the method on page 33 or the pizza dough on page 10. Shape the dough into a ball, sprinkle with flour and leave it to rise in the bowl, covered with a damp teatowel, for about 2 hours.

Punch the dough and knead for 1 minute. Roll out on a lightly floured surface to a thickness of 1cm (⅓ inch). (If you don't have a large table or bench on which to do this, roll out the dough in small batches.)

Pour the oil to a depth of 2–3cm (1 inch) in a large deep frying pan and heat. Test if it is hot enough by dropping in a little piece of dough – if the dough bubbles up and cooks quickly without burning the oil is hot enough. Cut the dough into pieces (use a pastry cutter if you like) and fry, turning once, until golden. As soon as each piece is cooked, quickly transfer it to a plate lined with kitchen paper to absorb excess oil.

Sprinkle with a little salt if you like and eat immediately.

Gnocco fritto is best eaten immediately, so I usually cook it and serve it to everybody sitting at the kitchen table, with a glass of wine and a nice piece of pecorino (sheep's cheese).

Tips and variations

✳ Leftover gnocco fritto can be enjoyed cold, in the children's lunchbox, or just lightly reheated. Some people make the dough using half water and half milk. My family also makes something similar called *paste fritte*, which involves mixing eggs and flour together (no yeast), similar to making fresh pasta, and then frying it.

Tortillas

My Mexican cousin Alejandro taught me how to make tortillas. He has a special tortilla press, so I have had to adapt his recipe so they can be easily made in an ordinary frying pan.

Ingredients

300g/10½oz high-grade flour, plus extra
    for dusting
30g/1oz butter, melted
100ml/3½fl oz very hot water
oil for frying

Makes 12 tortillas

Place the flour in a mixing bowl, then add the melted butter and the hot water and mix with a spoon. (The water must be very hot, almost boiling.) When the dough has cooled enough to touch, knead it well with one hand until it takes on a very smooth texture. Shape the dough into a ball, wrap it in cling film and leave it to rest for 30 minutes.

Divide the dough into 12 pieces and shape each into a small ball. Roll out each ball to form a disk the size of a CD. Lightly brush a frying pan with oil and heat. Cook the tortillas, one at a time, pressing them down with a wooden spoon so they cook evenly. As soon as they develop little brown spots underneath, flip and cook the other side. Brush the pan with oil before adding the next tortilla. Stack the cooked tortillas on a teatowel dusted with flour, and sprinkle flour between each layer to avoid them sticking together. Fold over the corners of the teatowel between each addition to keep them warm. When all the tortillas are cooked, serve as soon as possible with Mexican beans, salsa, cheese or your favourite fillings.

Tips and variations

* It is nice to have a helper: one person to roll the tortillas and another to cook.
* To make *quesadillas*, stuff the tortillas with grated cheese, fold in half and heat in the microwave or oven until the cheese has melted. Mexican white cheeses or mozzarella are best, but grated edam also works well.

Making Shortcrust Pastry - see page 56

Pastries & Pies

The definition of a pie is, generally speaking, a dish with a top on it (originally designed to keep the dish warm for longer). It can also feature a base *and* a top, effectively creating a container to hold a delicious filling, which can be eaten hot or cold. Using these loose definitions, I have created a number of pies for all occasions: rich and warming pies like Winter Vegetable Pie with Italian Potato Mash Topping or lighter and more picnic-style pies such as Easter Pie. In this chapter you will also find a great many pastry ideas that are perfect for pies, as well as the tarts and quiches in Chapter 4. More pastry varieties can be found in individual recipes, such as the Spicy Potato Strudel, making this chapter a truly useful one if you would like to experiment a bit more with 'out of the ordinary' fillings and toppings.

Butter Puff Pastry

There is nothing like homemade butter puff pastry – it tastes so much better than the frozen commercial varieties! However, as the butter/flour ratio is so cholesterol-laden, it's probably best that you save this delicacy for special occasions. And, as it takes some time to make, I suggest you make a big batch of pastry, cut it into pieces and freeze them. This pastry is best made when the weather is cooler.

Ingredients

500g/1lb 2oz high-grade flour
pinch of salt
250ml/8½fl oz water
1 x 500g/1lb 2oz block unsalted butter

Makes over 1kg (2lb 3oz)

Mix the flour with the salt and water in a large bowl. Knead well to make a soft and silky dough. Wrap the dough in cling film and leave to rest for 30 minutes.

In the meantime cut the butter in half lengthways, and set aside (keep at room temperature if it is winter or in a cool place, but not in the fridge if it is summer).

Roll out the dough (ideally on a marble or granite surface) into a rectangular shape. Place both pieces of butter side by side in the centre of the dough and fold over the sides to form an envelope. Roll out the dough a little, then fold 1 side over the other and roll again. Repeat this process on all 4 sides. (Note: if the weather is really hot you may need to refrigerate the dough for 30 minutes between each rolling process. To help you remember which side was last folded, work clockwise and make a small incision to indicate the side last folded.)

After the initial rolling and folding on each side, continue the process for as long as you like – the aim here is to make multi-layered pastry, just like *mille-feuille*, so it is up to you to decide how many layers you want. When you have finished, refrigerate the dough for 30 minutes before cutting it into pieces. I suggest you then weigh each piece, wrap it in cling film and label it accordingly before freezing until required.

Tips and variations

✳ Although this pastry is good enough to eat on its own, I tend to use it for a topping, rather than a base. It's also perfect for making special savoury bites such as Puff Pastry Cheese and Spice Fans (see page 103).

✳ To make a sweet version, add 1 teaspoon of caster sugar, or simply brush the pastry with water and sprinkle with caster sugar before baking.

Dairy-free Puff Pastry

Use margarine that is suitable for baking, such as palm oil margarine, available in both organic and healthfood stores.

Ingredients

500g/1lb 2oz high-grade flour
pinch of salt
200ml/7fl oz water
1 x 250g/9oz tub margarine

Makes about 1kg (2lb 3oz)

In a bowl mix half the flour with the salt and half the water. Knead well to make a soft and silky dough. Wrap the dough in cling film and leave to rest for 30 minutes.

In the meantime cut the margarine in half lengthways and set aside (keep at room temperature if it is winter or in a cool place, but not in the fridge, if it is summer).

Roll out the dough (ideally on a marble or granite surface) into a rectangular shape. Place both pieces of margarine side by side in the centre of the dough and fold over the sides to form an envelope. Roll out the dough a little, then fold 1 side over the other and roll again. Repeat this process on all 4 sides, then refrigerate. (Note: if the weather is really hot you may need to refrigerate the dough for 30 minutes between each rolling process. To help you remember which side was last folded, work clockwise and make a small incision to indicate the side last folded.)

Mix the remaining flour (250g/7oz) with the remaining water to make another batch of dough. Wrap in cling film and leave to rest for 30 minutes. Roll out the new dough into a rectangular shape, place the old dough inside and repeat the rolling and folding process on each side.

Continue rolling and folding to achieve as many layers as you like. When you have finished, refrigerate the dough for 30 minutes before cutting it into pieces. I suggest you then weigh each piece, wrap it in cling film and label it accordingly before freezing until required.

Tips and variations

✳ Use as regular puff pastry. The reason for making it in 2 steps is because margarine becomes more 'liquid' than butter when rolling, so introducing a second layer of dough that is folded over the first 'greasy' one will produce more pronounced layers of pastry.

Shortcrust Pastry

Shortcrust pastry is ideal for a variety of pies, quiches and other tarts. The following recipe makes approximately 400g (14oz) of pastry, which is enough to make the base and top of a 23cm (9 inch) pie or the base for 2 x 23cm (9 inch) quiches.

Ingredients

250g/9oz high-grade flour
pinch of salt
125g/4oz unsalted butter, chilled
   and cubed
1 egg
3 tablespoons cold water

Place the flour and salt in a large bowl. Add the cubed butter and mix with your hands. When the mixture is crumbly, add the egg and water and keep kneading until you get a smooth-textured mass. Roll out the pastry as required.

Tips and variations

* If making just 1 quiche, cut the pastry in half and wrap the other in cling film for later use (it will last for a couple of days in the fridge and up to 1 month in the freezer).
* Shortcrust pastry can also be made without an egg, just add 3 extra tablespoons of water.

Savoury Pastry

This is a less buttery variation of shortcrust pastry, suitable for more rustic types of pie and tart. The following recipe makes enough for the base and top of a 23cm (9 inch) pie or for the base of 2 x 23cm (9 inch) 'topless' tarts.

Ingredients

250g/9oz high-grade flour
pinch of salt
50g/2oz unsalted butter, chilled
   and cubed
1 egg
50ml/2fl oz cold water

Place the flour and salt in a large bowl. Add the cubed butter and mix with your hands. When the mixture is crumbly, add the egg and water and keep kneading until you get a smooth-textured mass. Roll out the pastry as required.

Tips and variations

* Replace the butter with margarine for a dairy-free variation. Add dried herbs or a little tomato paste for colour and a different taste.

Cabbage Filo Log

Inexpensive and nutritious, cabbage makes a great filling.

Ingredients

½ medium green cabbage
salt for sprinkling
1 tablespoon olive oil
2 medium carrots
300ml/10fl oz vegetable stock
1 tablespoon chopped parsley
pepper to taste
12 sheets filo pastry
olive oil spray or melted butter for
    brushing pastry
200g/17oz edam or gruyère cheese, sliced

Serves 6–8

Finely slice the cabbage, sprinkle with salt and leave it to rest for 15 minutes (this will reduce any bitterness). Rinse and drain the cabbage, then place in a large saucepan with the olive oil and cover. Simmer gently over a low heat for a few minutes.

In the meantime cut the carrots into fine strips and add to the cabbage. Pour in the stock and continue to simmer until all the vegetables are soft. Remove the lid and simmer for a further 10 minutes, stirring often, until all the liquid has evaporated. Stir in the parsley and pepper to taste and set aside.

Preheat the oven to 180°C (350°F).

Line a large oven tray with baking paper and cover with 2 sheets of filo pastry. Spray with oil or brush well with melted butter, top with 2 more sheets and brush with oil. Repeat this process until only 2 sheets are left. Spoon the cabbage mixture on top of the layered sheets to form a long rectangular shape (i.e. log-shaped). Cover with the cheese, then top with the 2 remaining sheets of filo. Lift the sides over the log and spray with oil to seal.

Bake for approximately 20 minutes or until the top is golden brown.

Serve hot.

Tips and variations

✳ Add whatever vegetables you like to the mixture – just be sure to slice them finely to make the log itself easier to slice.

Delicatessen Pie

Impress your guests with this amazingly tasty pie made with just a few ingredients from your local delicatessen or supermarket.

Ingredients

4 medium potatoes, boiled and peeled
100g/3½oz peas, cooked
100g/3½oz baby spinach or rocket leaves
200g/7oz cubed marinated feta cheese
10 sun-dried tomatoes in oil
12 pitted green and/or black olives
4 roasted capsicums (peppers)
olive oil (optional)
salt and pepper to taste
1 x quantity Savoury Pastry
   (see recipe on page 56)
1 egg

Serves 10–12

Cut the potatoes into small cubes and place in a large bowl with the peas and green leaves. Add the feta, sun-dried tomatoes, olives and capsicums, along with any oils/marinades from the delicatessen goods. Mix well and add a little more olive oil if desired. Season to taste and leave to rest for at least 30 minutes for the potatoes to better absorb the oil.

In the meantime, prepare the pastry according to the instructions on page 56.

Preheat the oven to 180°C (350°F)

Cut the pastry into 2 pieces, 1 slightly larger. Roll out the larger piece to fill a 23cm (9 inch) diameter well-greased flan dish (alternatively, line it with baking paper), allowing some pastry overhang. Fill with the potato mixture, spreading it out evenly. Make a small hole in the centre of the filling and break the egg into it. Roll out the second piece of pastry to make the top. Cover the pie with the pastry, sealing the edges and then rolling them to create a frame around the pie. Using the tip of a sharp knife, make a few incisions on the top to allow the steam to escape.

Bake for 30 minutes or until the crust is golden.

Serve hot or cold.

Tips and variations

✻ Vary the delicatessen ingredients as much as you like, e.g. marinated artichokes, *bocconcini* (bite-sized mozzarella cheeses), grilled eggplant (aubergine), etc. What you should aim to achieve is a delicious explosion of flavours!

Capsicum and Mozzarella Pie

My cooking class students tell me they love this pie because it is so quick and easy!

Ingredients

3 large capsicums (peppers), yellow,
   red and green
1 celery stalk with leaves
1 tablespoon olive oil
100ml/3½fl oz vegetable stock
1 tablespoon tomato paste
2 x 160g/5½oz ready-rolled puff
   pastry sheets
salt and pepper to taste
small handful of fresh basil leaves
1 fresh mozzarella or edam cheese,
   thinly sliced

Serves 4

Remove the seeds from the capsicums and cut the flesh into thin slices. Chop the celery (leaves included) into small pieces. Heat the oil in a large frying pan and sauté the vegetables for a few seconds. Add the vegetable stock and tomato paste. Simmer for 15 minutes, stirring from time to time.

In the meantime thaw the ready-rolled puff pastry sheets at room temperature. Preheat the oven to 180°C (350°F).

Check the vegetables in the pan and when all the liquid has evaporated season to taste, and stir through the basil leaves.

Place 1 pastry sheet on an oven tray lined with baking paper. Spread over the capsicum mixture, leaving the outside edges uncovered. Top with the sliced cheese and cover with the second sheet of pastry, sealing the edges well.

Bake for 20 minutes or until the pastry is golden and perfectly cooked.

Remove from the oven and allow to cool for 5 minutes before slicing.

Tips and variations

* Eggplants (aubergines) and courgettes (zucchini) also work well in this pie.

Easter Pie

In Italy, spinach and eggs are symbolic of spring. Use frozen spinach to make this pie all year round.

Ingredients

500g/1lb 2oz frozen spinach
50g/2oz butter
1 clove garlic, peeled and finely sliced
salt and pepper to taste
pinch of freshly ground nutmeg
1 x quantity Savoury Pastry
  (see recipe on page 56)
10 eggs

Serves 10

Thaw the spinach. In a large frying pan melt the butter over a low heat. Add the garlic and the thawed spinach and simmer for a few minutes until all the water from the spinach has evaporated. Add salt, pepper and nutmeg to taste, then set aside.

In the meantime, prepare the pastry according to the instructions on page 56.

Preheat the oven to 180°C (350°F). Cut the pastry into 2 pieces, 1 slightly larger. Roll out the larger piece to fill a 23cm (9 inch) diameter well-greased flan dish (alternatively, line it with baking paper), allowing some pastry overhang. Fill with the spinach mixture, spreading it out evenly. Using your fingers, make 10 depressions in the mixture in a circle shape close to the edge of the pie. Break an egg into each hole.

Roll out the second piece of pastry to make the top. Cover the pie with the pastry, sealing the edges and then rolling them to create a frame around the pie. Using the tip of a sharp knife, make a few incisions on the top to allow the steam to escape.

Bake for 30 minutes or until the crust is golden. Serve hot or cold.

Tips and variations

✻ Add some ricotta cheese and/or parmesan to the spinach mixture.

Eggplant Terrine

You will need to use very large eggplants (aubergines) for this dish, which is best made during the summer months when these vegetables are plentiful.

Ingredients

2 very large eggplants (aubergines)
salt for sprinkling
olive oil for brushing
1 medium onion
4 tablespoons olive oil
salt to taste
12 cherry tomatoes
small handful of basil leaves
3 tablespoons breadcrumbs

Serves 6

Cut the eggplants in half lengthways, then carefully cut 4–5 very thin lengthways slices from each half so that you have 16–20 in total. Set aside in a large colander. Chop the remaining eggplant flesh into small cubes and add to the colander. Sprinkle with salt and leave to sweat for 30 minutes. Rinse well and pat dry.

Transfer the long slices to an oven tray (leave the cubes in the colander for now). Brush the slices with olive oil, sprinkle with just a little salt and grill on both sides until soft.

In the meantime peel and finely chop the onion. Heat 2 tablespoons of the olive oil in a large frying pan and sauté the onion until soft and shiny. Add the cubed eggplant, cherry tomatoes and a pinch of salt and stir. Cover and simmer for about 10 minutes. Taste for salt, then turn off heat. Add the basil leaves, the remaining 2 tablespoons of oil and the breadcrumbs. Stir and set aside. The mixture should be quite dry; if it is too soggy add some more breadcrumbs.

Preheat the oven to 180°C (350°F).

Line a 23 x 13cm (9 x 5 inch) loaf tin with baking paper. Line again with the grilled eggplant strips, leaving a few for the top. Spoon in the vegetable mixture, pressing it down firmly with a spoon. Cover with the remaining eggplant strips, folding any overhanging strips towards the centre to cover and seal the terrine. Cover with a sheet of baking paper cut to size.

Bake for approximately 30 minutes. Remove from the oven and allow to cool for 5–10 minutes. Reverse the tin onto a serving plate, peel off the baking paper and serve. For best results, slice with a serrated knife.

Tips and variations

✱ Add a few pitted black olives and/or capers. Substitute tomatoes with red capsicum (pepper), or basil with fresh marjoram. Add a little chilli or paprika. For a wheat-free alternative, replace the breadcrumbs with ground nuts.

Erbazzone

Typical of the Northern Italian region of Emilia Romagna where I come from, *erbazzone* can be found in all the local bakeries. Each family has its own recipe for this pie, many of which include the local lard, both in the pastry and the filling. But as this product is difficult to find outside Emilia Romagna, let alone Italy, I use butter instead.

Ingredients

FILLING
120g/4oz silverbeet, white stalks
   removed
120g/4oz spinach
1 large shallot or 1 small onion
50g/2oz butter
salt to taste

PASTRY
200g/7oz high-grade flour, plus extra
   for sprinkling
pinch of salt
50g/2oz butter, chilled and cubed
100ml/3½fl oz cold water

Serves 4–6

Wash the silverbeet and spinach, then chop into small strips. Peel and finely slice the shallot.

Heat the butter in a large saucepan and sauté the shallot until translucent. Add the salt, then the chopped greens and simmer, covered, for 15 minutes, stirring from time to time. When the greens have reduced, remove the lid and cook until all the liquid has evaporated (about 15 more minutes). Set aside while you make the pastry.

Place the flour and salt in a large bowl. Add the butter and mix with your hands until the mixture is crumbly. Add the water and keep kneading until you get a smooth-textured mass. Divide the pastry into 2 equal pieces. Lightly flour the benchtop and using a rolling pin, roll out each piece into a disk shape.

Preheat the oven to 180°C (350°F).

Transfer 1 disc to an oven tray lined with baking paper. Spread over the cooked greens, leaving the outside edge uncovered. Cover with the second disc and seal the edges by pinching them with your fingers or using a pastry cutter.

Bake for approximately 25–30 minutes.

Serve hot or cold.

Tips and variations

✳ The word *erbazzone* comes from *erba*, which is Italian for grass. In spring, especially in the mountains, a lot of wild greens are collected from the fields and all of it goes into the *erbazzone*: dandelion leaves, chicory and other bitter leaves are particularly loved by Italians. If you wish, you can use olive oil instead of butter in both the pastry and the filling for a dairy-free option.

Polenta Bomb

Polenta makes a great shell or topping for wheat-free pies and this recipe makes enough to feed an army!
As you become more skilful, you can make lots of small individual 'bombs' of different shapes.

Ingredients

FILLING
1kg/2lb 2oz courgettes (zucchini)
1 onion
2 tablespoons olive oil
1 x 400g/14oz can Italian peeled tomatoes
pinch of dried oregano
1 small dried red chilli
1 tablespoon chopped sun-dried tomatoes
1 tablespoon tomato paste
salt to taste
1 tablespoon chopped parsley
1 mozzarella cheese, cubed (optional)

SHELL
500g polenta
salt to taste
butter for greasing the mould/s

Serves 12

Wash the courgettes and cut into thick slices. Peel and finely chop the onion. Heat the olive oil in a large frying pan. Add the prepared vegetables and sauté for 5 minutes. Stir through the canned tomatoes, breaking them up as you stir. Add the oregano, chilli, sun-dried tomatoes and the tomato paste. Simmer, stirring often, until the sauce thickens. Season to taste and add the chopped parsley.

Prepare the polenta according to the instructions on the packet (if you use instant polenta it will take only 5 minutes from boiling point, otherwise it takes about 40 minutes).

Preheat the oven to 180°C (350°F).

Grease a large ovenproof bowl (Pyrex is ideal) with butter and pour in half the hot polenta. Move the bowl in order to spread the polenta evenly around the sides (as it sets quickly you will need to work fast).

Add the mozzarella to the courgette mixture if using, then slowly pour the mixture into the centre of the bowl. As this action will push the polenta up the sides, ensure that a thick layer stays at the bottom of the bowl. Spoon the remaining polenta on top of the courgette mixture to seal the bomb (save any unused polenta for another time).

Bake for 15 minutes, then tip out over a large serving plate. Voilá, your polenta bomb is ready.

Slice and serve hot with extra butter and parmesan cheese if desired.

Tips and variations

* You can use any pie filling as long as it is not too runny. Mushrooms in particular are deliciously compatible with polenta. Or you could put the filling in a pie dish, then top with slices of polenta and grated cheese. Or make a polenta lasagne by alternating thin slices of polenta with layers of filling.
* Fry leftover pieces of polenta in a little olive oil flavoured with garlic and rosemary. Or grill or barbecue and top with cheese or grilled vegetables.

Spanakopita

No chapter on pies would be complete without a recipe for Spanakopita. It is one of my favourite pies and I make it often, with many variations.

Ingredients

1kg/2lb 2oz fresh spinach
salt for sprinkling
1 medium onion
1 tablespoon olive oil
400g/14oz goat's feta cheese
1 teaspoon dried oregano
pepper to taste
200g/7oz butter
1 x 375g/13oz packet chilled filo pastry

Serves 6–8

Wash the spinach thoroughly. Roughly chop the leaves, remove the stalks and chop coarsely. Place the leaves in a large colander and sprinkle with salt. Set aside for 30 minutes to reduce in size, then rinse well under cold water and drain. (If time is short, simply wilt the leaves in boiling water for a few seconds and drain.) Peel and finely slice the onion. Heat the oil in a frying pan and sauté the onion until soft and translucent.

In a large bowl crumble the feta cheese. Add the spinach leaves and stalks, the cooked onion, oregano and pepper, and mix well. Taste to check if more salt is needed, although the feta makes it quite salty.

Melt the butter in a small bowl and place it inside a larger bowl half-filled with hot water to avoid the butter solidifying again. This will be used to brush the filo pastry.

Preheat the oven to 180°C (350°F).

Line a large oven tray with baking paper and cover with 2 sheets of filo pastry. Brush the top sheet with some melted butter. Cover with 2 more sheets and repeat the process until there are about 8 sheets of pastry left. Spread the spinach and feta mixture over the buttered sheets leaving the outside edges uncovered. Cover with the remaining filo pastry sheets, 2 at a time, brushing the top sheet with butter each time. Seal the edges well.

Bake for approximately 50 minutes or until the top is golden brown.

Tips and variations

✳ I prefer to use chilled filo pastry (look for it in the delicatessen fridge at the supermarket) rather than the frozen kind because the latter tends to break more easily.
✳ You can use cow's feta rather than goat's for a change, and perhaps garlic and crushed cumin seeds instead of oregano.
✳ When time allows, I roll little individual filo parcels rather than make one large pie.

Vegetable Crumble with Blue Cheese Sauce

A warming vegetable crumble featuring Brussels sprouts for cold winter nights. I've deliberately used sprouts to show how easy it can be to transform this often less-than-popular vegetable into a tasty meal.

Ingredients

FILLING
500g/1lb 1oz potatoes
2 medium carrots
1 celery stalk with leaves
3 tablespoons olive oil
1 clove garlic, sliced
500ml/17fl oz vegetable stock
500g/1lb 1oz Brussels sprouts
salt and pepper to taste
1 tablespoon chopped parsley

TOPPING
200g/7oz breadcrumbs
50g/2oz butter, cubed

SAUCE
1 tablespoon plain flour
250ml/8½fl oz milk
125g/4oz blue cheese, crumbled
salt and pepper to taste
1 tablespoon chopped parsley

Serves 8

Peel the potatoes and cut into large chunks. Roughly slice the carrots and celery. Heat the oil in a very large frying pan or casserole dish. Add the garlic and the chopped vegetables and sauté quickly for 2 minutes. Pour in the stock, cover and simmer for a few minutes.

In the meantime, clean and chop the Brussels sprouts (unless they are really small). When the potatoes are half cooked, add the Brussels sprouts and continue cooking. When the vegetables are cooked and the stock has just about been absorbed, turn off the heat. Season to taste and add the chopped parsley.

To make the topping, mix the breadcrumbs with the butter until well combined. Preheat the oven to 180°C (350°F).

Spoon the vegetable filling into a suitable pie or lasagne dish and spread the crumble evenly on top.

Bake for approximately 30 minutes or until the crumble is golden.

To make the sauce, place the flour with a little of the milk into a saucepan and mix well, ensuring there are no lumps. Add the rest of the milk and bring to the boil, stirring continuously. When the sauce thickens, add the cheese and stir through to melt. Turn off the heat, season to taste and add the chopped parsley.

Serve hot with the sauce on the side.

Tips and variations

✳ The strength and quality of the cheese will greatly affect the taste of the sauce. However, if you or your family is not keen on blue cheese, use grated cheddar or edam cheese instead and substitute chives for the parsley.

Spicy Potato Strudel

Potatoes are such versatile and nutritious vegetables that I think they should star at the dinner table, rather than end up as side dishes. It's possible to make the dough and the filling for this recipe one day ahead.

Ingredients

FILLING
500g/1lb 1oz old potatoes
1 medium onion
1 medium carrot
1 tablespoon vegetable oil
1 teaspoon curry powder
100ml/3½fl oz hot vegetable stock
salt to taste
1 tablespoon roughly chopped coriander
   or parsley

PASTRY
50g/2oz margarine or butter, cubed
200g/7oz high-grade flour
pinch of salt
100ml/3½fl oz water

Serves 4

Peel the potatoes and cut into small cubes, then pat dry with a teatowel. Peel and finely chop the onion and carrot using a large knife or a *mezzaluna* (Italian half-moon chopping knife).

Heat the oil in a large frying pan. Add the curry powder and the chopped vegetables. Sauté for 2 minutes, stirring regularly, then add the hot stock and cover. Simmer for about 10 minutes, then uncover and continue cooking, still stirring, until all the stock has been absorbed. The vegetables should be quite dry. Taste to check if the mixture needs salt, then add the chopped coriander. Set aside to cool.

To make the pastry, place the margarine, flour and salt into a large bowl and mix with your fingers. Add the water and work into a soft dough. Wrap the dough in cling film and chill in the refrigerator for at least 30 minutes.

Preheat the oven to 180°C (350°F).

On a lightly floured surface roll out the dough as thinly as possible. Spread the cold filling over the dough and start folding the pastry over the mixture to make a large roll. Halfway through the process, fold the edges in as if you were making a spring roll so that the strudel is well sealed.

Transfer the strudel to an oven tray lined with baking paper.

Bake for approximately 50 minutes.

Serve hot or cold.

Tips and variations

✴ For more colour, add peas or chopped green beans or a few cherry tomatoes to the other vegetables before sautéing.
✴ Replace the curry powder with your own mix of spices.

Winter Vegetable Pie with Italian Potato Mash Topping

Here are two recipes in one: a warming and filling pie ideal for winter, and a topping made with *purè di patate* (Italian mashed potatoes) that will forever change the way you cook your mash.

Ingredients

TOPPING
about 750g/1lb 10oz old potatoes
500ml/17fl oz milk
50g/2oz butter
salt and freshly ground pepper to taste
pinch of freshly grated nutmeg
2 tablespoons grated parmesan cheese

FILLING
2 large leeks
1 large carrot
2 celery stalks with leaves
1 small potato
2 tablespoons olive oil
250ml/8½fl oz hot vegetable stock
300g/10½oz frozen peas
salt and pepper to taste

Serves 6

Wash the potatoes but do not peel or chop, then cook in plenty of water.

To make the filling, wash the leeks and cut into thick chunks, using as much of the green part as possible. Slice the carrots and celery stalks into small rounds and chop the celery leaves. Peel the small potato and cut into very small cubes (so small they will practically melt during cooking thus thickening the sauce).

Heat the oil in a large frying pan, then add the chopped vegetables. Sauté for 2 minutes, stirring continuously, then add the hot stock. Cover and simmer for about 15 minutes, then add the frozen peas. Cover and continue cooking for a further 5 minutes. Remove the lid and stir, season to taste and set aside to cool.

By this time the whole potatoes for the topping should be cooked. Prick them with a fork to check and when they are ready, drain, peel and mash them, ideally using a potato ricer, which looks like a large garlic press and makes the potatoes light and fluffy. Transfer the mash to a saucepan and add the milk. Stir, then add the butter. Simmer, stirring often, until the mash thickens (about 15–20 minutes). Add salt, pepper and nutmeg to taste.

Preheat the oven to 180°C (350°F).

Pour the cooked vegetable mixture into a high-sided pie or lasagne dish (preferably non-metallic). Spread the mashed potatoes evenly on top and sprinkle with the parmesan cheese.

Bake for approximately 35–40 minutes or until the crust is golden. Remove from the oven and allow to cool for 5 minutes before serving.

Tips and variations

* Experiment with different vegetables, e.g. onions, swedes, turnips, frozen green beans, etc – the possibilities are endless. Leeks, with their sweet and distinctive flavour, are best left uncompromised so don't add any herbs. But if you replace leeks with onions, their taste would greatly benefit from the addition of a few sage leaves.

Cheese and Walnut Tart – see page 82

Flans, Quiches & Savoury Tarts

Although they are very popular these days, flans, quiches and tarts often seem so complicated to make that many of us tend to purchase them ready-made, rather than making them at home. But it's just a matter of learning a few tricks that will have you up and running in no time ready to start inventing your own masterpieces. Some of these recipes are wonderfully colourful, too, making them suitable as ornamental centrepieces for the table as well as being delicious to eat, for example Red Beetroot and Feta Tart, and Cherry Tomato Quiche.

Artichoke Flan with Artichoke Sauce

A rich and sophisticated main course for the most discerning of diners, this is one of my favourite creations.

Ingredients

FLAN
juice of 1 medium lemon
2 large globe artichokes
2 cloves garlic, peeled
handful of Italian (flat-leaf) parsley
1 teaspoon rock salt
2 tablespoons extra virgin olive oil
160g/5½oz Butter Puff Pastry
   (see page 54) or use bought pastry
extra chopped parsley for decorating

SAUCE
1 tablespoon plain flour
20g/1oz butter
salt and pepper to taste
1 tablespoon chopped parsley

Serves 4

Fill a mixing bowl with water and add the lemon juice (throw in the lemon shells for extra juice). Cut the stalks off the artichokes (if they are the thorny type, remove any thorns with scissors). Quickly transfer the artichokes to the bowl of lemon water or they will turn black.

Combine the garlic cloves with the parsley and rock salt and chop, using a large kitchen knife or a *mezzaluna* (Italian half-moon knife).

Remove the artichokes from the lemon water and, using your fingers, open the centre of each to reveal the heart. Stuff the centre with the parsley mixture and place, face up, in a saucepan. Pour the olive oil into the artichoke hearts, and then fill the pan with water to halfway cover the artichokes. Cover and simmer for about 45 minutes or until the outer leaves detach easily. Drain, reserving the liquid for later use. Remove the outer leaves from the artichokes, also reserving these for later use. Cut each artichoke into two lengthways and set aside.

To make the sauce, scrape all the flesh from the outer leaves (discard the hard bits). Blend the flesh with the cooking juices until smooth, then place in a saucepan with the flour and stir, ensuring there are no lumps. Bring to the boil and simmer for about 5 minutes until the sauce thickens, then add the butter and cook for a further few minutes until when you taste it, you cannot detect a floury after-taste. Add salt and pepper to taste, followed by the chopped parsley. Keep warm.

Preheat the oven to 180°C (350°F).

To make the flan, roll out the pastry to form a 25–30cm (10–12 inch) square. Transfer to an oven tray lined with baking paper and place the artichoke halves on it.

Bake for 15 minutes or until the pastry turns golden brown and has puffed up around the artichokes.

To assemble, cut the pastry into 4 ensuring that each piece has its own artichoke half, and serve accompanied by the sauce and your favourite vegetables.

Tips and variations

✱ Leftover sauce will enrich any dish, but it should be served hot or warm. If you prefer, use canned artichoke hearts for the flan, in which case you will need to make a different sauce (perhaps some kind of gravy) to go with it.

Brie and Mushroom Tart

A very tasty and easy dish to serve at your next dinner party.

Ingredients

200g/7oz champignon (button) or
  similar mushrooms
25g/1oz butter
salt and pepper to taste
200g/7oz brie
50ml/2fl oz milk
2 eggs
1 tablespoon finely chopped parsley
200g/7oz Shortcrust Pastry
  (see page 56)

Serves 8–10

Clean and slice the mushrooms.

Melt the butter in a frying pan, add the mushrooms and sauté for 5 minutes. Season to taste and set aside.

Process the brie and milk in a blender until creamy. In a large mixing bowl whisk the eggs. Fold in the milk mixture and chopped parsley.

Preheat the oven to 180°C (350°F).

Line a 23cm (9 inch) shallow round flan dish with baking paper. Roll out the pastry to fit the base and sides of the flan dish. Cover the base with the cooked mushrooms, then pour over the brie mixture.

Bake for approximately 30 minutes or until the pastry turns golden brown and the filling has set. Remove from the oven and allow to cool for about 1 hour.

Tips and variations

✳ Replace mushrooms with sliced sautéd courgettes or uncooked courgette flowers.

Asparagus and Parmigiano Quiche

Asparagus and Parmigiano Reggiano cheese is a match made in heaven!

Ingredients

15–20 asparagus spears
4 eggs
250ml/8½fl oz single or double cream
2 tablespoons grated Parmigiano
  Reggiano cheese
salt and pepper to taste
200g/7oz Shortcrust Pastry
  (see page 56)

Serves 8–10

Clean the asparagus and cut or break off the tough ends and discard. Cut off the tips and set aside. Cut the green stalks into small slices. Quickly blanch the tips and slices in boiling water for 30 seconds, then set aside.

Using an electric beater, whisk the eggs with the cream. Add the cheese and season to taste. Fold in the sliced asparagus including the tips.

Preheat the oven to 180°C (350°F).

Line a 23cm (9 inch) round flan dish with baking paper.

Roll out the pastry to fit the base and sides of the flan dish. Pour in the egg and asparagus mixture.

Bake for approximately 30 minutes or until the pastry turns golden brown and the filling has set.

Serve cold or gently reheated.

Tips and variations

✳ Replace the asparagus with other green vegetables. Make a spring quiche by combining fresh asparagus with cherry tomatoes and baby peas.

Brussels Sprouts Flan

Do you find it hard to swallow those Brussels sprouts? Here is an easy flan that, surprise surprise, grown-ups *and* children will enjoy.

Ingredients

500g/1lb 1oz Brussels sprouts
salt
200ml/7fl oz vegetable stock
160g/5½oz Butter Puff Pastry
    (see page 54) or use bought pastry
100g/3½oz grated mild cheese

Serves 4

Clean the Brussels sprouts, removing stalks and any damaged outer leaves from the sprouts. Cut in half (unless they are very small) and place in a colander. Sprinkle with salt and leave to rest for 30 minutes. Rinse well with cold water, drain, and place in a large saucepan with the vegetable stock. Cook, covered, on low heat for approximately 15 minutes or until all the stock has been absorbed. If there is still some stock left, remove the lid and cook, uncovered, for a further 5 minutes. Set aside to cool.

Preheat the oven to 180°C (350°F).

Line a 23cm (9 inch) round flan dish with baking paper. Roll out the pastry to fit the base and sides of the flan dish. Place another sheet of baking paper on top of the pastry and fill with dried beans or baking weights.

Blind bake for 15 minutes. Remove the beans and paper, then arrange the Brussels sprouts, cut-side down, in a circular pattern, much as you would for a fruit tart. Sprinkle with the cheese and return to the oven for a further 15 minutes or until the pastry turns golden brown.

Serve hot or cold.

Tips and variations

✳ Try making this flan with any other vegetables that your family may dislike (e.g. cooked spinach, kale, silverbeet, broccoli and cauliflower). Cooked in this flan, they will soon become favourites!

✳ Add chopped tomatoes, mozzarella and dried oregano for a *pizzaiola-style* flan.

Cheese and Spring Onion Quiche

A twist on the classic cheese and onion combination, I find this quiche a better option because it's more delicate and colourful, and you need just a small amount of spring onions.

Ingredients

4 eggs
200ml/7fl oz single or double cream
salt and pepper to taste
1 tablespoon chopped spring onion, plus extra for decoration
200g/7oz Shortcrust Pastry (see page 56)
100g/3½oz grated edam or gruyère cheese

Serves 10

Using an electric beater, whisk the eggs with the cream. Season to taste and fold in the spring onions.

Preheat the oven to 180°C (350°F).

Line a 23cm (9 inch) round flan dish with baking paper. Roll out the pastry to fit the base and sides of the flan dish. Sprinkle the grated cheese over the base and pour in the egg mixture.

Bake for approximately 30 minutes or until the pastry turns golden brown and the filling has set.

Serve cold, garnished with chopped spring onions.

Tips and variations

* Absolutely delicious with finely chopped chives instead of spring onions (my favourite variation). Also great with cherry tomatoes, basil leaves, grated courgette (zucchini) or simply any vegetable at hand!

Cherry Tomato Quiche

You need really flavoursome cherry tomatoes for this quiche. Homegrown tomatoes are best, even if they come from a modest pot on the deck!

Ingredients

4 eggs
200ml/7fl oz single or double cream
1 tablespoon grated Parmigiano
   Reggiano cheese
salt and pepper to taste
25–30 sun-ripened cherry tomatoes
pinch of dried oregano
200g/7oz Shortcrust Pastry
   (see page 56) or
   Savoury Pastry (page 56)
fresh oregano or basil for garnishing

Serves 10

Using an electric beater whisk the eggs with the cream. Add the grated cheese and season to taste.

Preheat the oven to 180°C (350°F).

Line a 23cm (9 inch) round flan dish with baking paper. Roll out the pastry to fit the base and sides of the flan dish. Pour in the egg mixture and arrange the cherry tomatoes on top, pushing them down into the mixture. Sprinkle with the dried oregano.

Bake for approximately 30 minutes or until the pastry turns golden brown and the filling has set.

Serve cold, garnished with fresh oregano or basil leaves.

Tips and variations

✳ While you can enjoy this quiche hot, just remember that the tomatoes will be extremely hot and could burn your mouth! If you don't have enough cherry tomatoes at hand, add a few pitted olives – they will add colour and taste.

Rocket Quiche

A classic quiche recipe enriched with the peppery addition of fragrant rocket leaves.

Ingredients

4 eggs
300ml/10fl oz single or double cream
50g/2oz grated Parmigiano
   Reggiano cheese
salt and pepper to taste
50g/2oz rocket leaves
200g/7oz Shortcrust Pastry
   (see page 56)

Serves 8–10

Using an electric beater, whisk the eggs in a large mixing bowl with the cream. Add the grated cheese and season to taste. Fold in the well-washed and dried rocket leaves.

Preheat the oven to 180°C (350°F).

Line a 23cm (9 inch) round flan dish with baking paper.

Roll out the pastry to fit the base and sides of the flan dish. Pour in the egg and rocket mixture.

Bake for approximately 30 minutes or until the pastry turns golden brown and the filling has set.

Serve cold or gently reheated.

Tips and variations

✳ Use baby spinach leaves instead of rocket. Other suitable vegetables include thinly sliced white onion, cherry tomatoes, grilled capsicum (pepper) strips, or just a handful of chopped mixed herbs.

Cheese and Walnut Tart

This cheese and walnut tart makes use of all those bits and pieces of cheese that tend to lurk in the refrigerator, so feel free to be very flexible about which kinds of cheese you use.

Ingredients

200g/7oz ricotta cheese
4 eggs
50g/2oz grated parmesan, pecorino or
   any hard cheese
50g/2oz any cheese, cubed or crumbled
salt and pepper to taste
2 tablespoons finely chopped parsley
20 whole walnut kernels
200g/7oz Shortcrust Pastry
   (see page 56)

Serves 8–10

In a large mixing bowl mix the ricotta with the eggs. Add all the cheese, salt and pepper, and the chopped parsley.

Preheat the oven to 180°C (350°F).

Line a 23cm (9 inch) round flan dish with baking paper.

Roll out the pastry to fit the base and sides of the flan dish. Pour in the cheese mixture, then arrange the walnut kernels on top, pressing them down slightly.

Bake for approximately 30 minutes or until the pastry turns golden brown and the filling has set.

Best served lukewarm or cold, or reheated later.

Tips and variations

✳ Different cheeses will affect the flavour; goat's feta or blue cheese are among my favourites, but even a mild cheese will produce a good result.
✳ Replace the parsley with a few whole rocket leaves.

Red Beetroot and Feta Tart

Beetroot is such a beautiful colour that it deserves to be treated as the main ingredient now and then. Here is a tart that looks so spectacular it could easily be mistaken for a cake.

Ingredients

400g/14oz medium beetroot
200g/7oz crumbly feta cheese
3 eggs
salt and pepper to taste
250g/9oz Shortcrust Pastry
    (see page 56)

Serves 8–10

Peel the raw beetroot and grate (best done in a food processor). Transfer to a bowl and crumble the feta on top. Mix well and allow to stand for a couple of hours so the flavours can mix.

In a separate bowl whisk the eggs with a fork. Season to taste (not too much – the feta can be quite salty), then add to the beetroot mixture.

Preheat the oven to 180°C (350°F).

Line a 23cm (9 inch) round flan dish with baking paper.

Roll out the pastry to fit the base and sides of the flan dish, reserving some to make criss-cross strips to cover the flan.

Pour the beetroot mixture into the pastry shell. Arrange the reserved strips to make a criss-cross pattern on top.

Bake for approximately 30 minutes or until the pastry turns golden brown and the filling has set.

Serve hot or cold.

Tips and variations

* Add 1 teaspoon of crushed cumin seeds for more zest.
* Use half grated beetroot and half grated carrot.
* Replace feta with ricotta cheese plus 2 tablespoons of grated spicy pecorino cheese.
* Add 1 tablespoon of chopped parsley to the beetroot and feta mixture.

Red Onion Flan

Here is an incredibly easy recipe for a fragrant red onion flan that takes very little time and effort to prepare.

Ingredients

1 large red onion
2 tablespoons olive oil
salt to taste
160g/5½oz Butter Puff Pastry
   (see page 54) or use bought puff pastry
3 eggs
freshly ground black pepper to taste
1 heaped tablespoon self-raising flour
3 tablespoons grated edam cheese
sprig of fresh thyme

Serves 4

Peel and finely slice the onion. Heat the oil in a frying pan and sauté the onion with a pinch of salt on low heat for 6–7 minutes, stirring regularly, until the onion is soft, but not coloured. Set aside to cool.

Roll out the pastry to fill the base and sides of a 23cm (9 inch) round flan dish lined with baking paper.

Preheat the oven to 180°C (350°F).

Beat the eggs with a pinch of salt, the ground pepper and the flour. Fold in the cooked onion, grated cheese and a few thyme leaves. Pour the mixture into the pastry shell.

Bake for 30 minutes.

Serve hot or cold.

Tips and variations

✳ Although brown and white onions can also be used in this recipe, I think red onions have more zest.
✳ Replace the thyme leaves with some sage; tear a few leaves with your fingers and sauté them with the onion.
✳ This flan serves 4 as a main, but is particularly suitable for cutting into very thin slices and serving in a buffet or as an appetiser.

Lentil Tart

This lentil tart, in which sliced potato forms the shell, is dairy-, egg- *and* wheat-free, making it the perfect dish to serve when feeding those with food allergies.

Ingredients

250g/9oz brown lentils
1 onion
1 carrot
1 stalk celery
2 cloves garlic
2 tablespoons olive oil
1 small red chilli (optional)
sprig of fresh thyme
600ml/20fl oz water, plus extra as needed
2 medium potatoes
salt and pepper to taste
fresh herbs to decorate

Serves 8–10

Rinse the lentils and soak them for about 4 hours.

In the meantime peel the onion and scrub the carrot. Chop finely along with the celery and garlic (use a food processor if you like).

Heat the olive oil in a frying pan and add the chilli, if using, followed by the chopped vegetables and sauté for 5 minutes. Stir through the drained lentils, add the thyme and then the water. Cover and simmer, stirring from time to time, until the lentils are cooked. Add a little more water if necessary, although the final product should look like a very thick soup, rather than too dry.

In the meantime, peel and thinly slice the potatoes (the thinner the better).

Preheat the oven to 180°C (350°F).

Line a 23cm (9 inch) round flan dish with baking paper.

Cover the bottom and sides of the lined dish with potato slices, dampening them if necessary so they will stick to the sides. Gently pour the lentil filling over the potato and spread it evenly. Remove the chilli at this point (unless you want to leave it in as a surprise for someone!). Season to taste.

Bake for approximately 30 minutes until the filling looks set.

Remove from the oven and allow to cool before lifting, paper and all, from the dish, at which point the potatoes will set around the filling – just like a pastry shell!

Decorate with fresh herb leaves just before serving.

Tips and Variations

✳ Use other types of lentils. Red lentils will not need soaking, just rinse them well to remove any impurities.

Torta Rustica

In Italy there are numerous variations on this dish, which translates as 'rustic tart'. In my version, I use an easy instant pastry that does not require rolling out. You can use this pastry to make your own variations on the rustic theme. It's important to weigh the greens after they've been cooked.

Ingredients

FILLING
300g/10½ oz cooked green leaves
   (e.g. spinach, rocket, silverbeet,
   chicory or a mixture of these)
200g/7oz feta cheese, crumbled
½ teaspoon cumin seeds
2 cloves garlic
2 ripe medium tomatoes
salt and pepper to taste

PASTRY
100g/3½oz butter, cubed
200g/7oz self-raising flour
pinch of salt
1 egg

Serves 8–10

Squeeze out most of the water from the cooked green leaves (leaving in enough so the leaves remain moist), and chop finely. Transfer the chopped greens to a large mixing bowl and mix in the crumbled feta cheese.

Coarsely grind the cumin seed, ideally using a mortar and pestle, and stir through the greens. Peel and crush the garlic and add to the greens. Cut the tomatoes over the bowl so you don't lose any juice and add to the mixture. Season to taste and set aside.

To make the pastry, place the butter, flour and salt in a large mixing bowl. Mix well until it crumbles between your fingers. Add the egg and, still using your fingers, work the dough for about 10 minutes or until it becomes smooth and soft.

Preheat the oven to 180°C (350°F).

Line a 23cm (9 inch) round flan dish with baking paper. Place the dough in the centre and push it down and outwards with your fingers until it covers the base and sides of the dish. Pour in the filling, spreading it evenly in the dish, then ease any overhanging edges of the pastry towards the centre of the tart. Bake for approximately 30 minutes or until the pastry is golden brown and the filling has set.

Allow the tart to cool a little before cutting or serve cold.

Tips and variations

* Anything goes here, i.e. the quantity of greens can depend on what is in the garden or the fridge the day you make the tart.
* Substitute cream cheese or ricotta for feta for a milder flavour.

Fennel and Ricotta Tart

This is a very sophisticated tart in which the distinctive flavour of fennel marries well with the lightness of ricotta.

Ingredients

10 baby fennel bulbs or 1 large
  Florence fennel, sliced
150ml/5fl oz vegetable stock
200g/7oz Shortcrust Pastry
  (see page 56)
250g/9oz ricotta cheese
3 eggs
2 teaspoons grated Parmigiano
  Reggiano cheese
salt and pepper to taste

Serves 10

Wash the fennel, remove stalks and save the leaves for garnish.

Place the fennel in a saucepan with the vegetable stock. Cover and simmer for 15 minutes. Remove the lid and simmer for a few more minutes until all the liquid has evaporated.

In the meantime line a 23cm (9 inch) round flan dish with baking paper.

Roll out the pastry to fit the base and sides of the flan dish.

Beat the ricotta with the eggs, cheese, salt and pepper, ideally using an electric beater.

Preheat the oven to 180°C (350°F).

Pour the ricotta mixture into the pastry shell and arrange the fennel on top, lightly pressing them down into the filling.

Bake for approximately 30 minutes or until the pastry is golden brown and the filling has risen like a soufflé.

Remove from the oven and allow to cool completely before slicing (the filling will settle back down during the cooling process).

Decorate with fennel leaves and serve cold or lightly reheated.

Tips and variations

* Use commercial savoury pastry to save time.
* Many other vegetables can be used with this ricotta filling including courgettes (zucchini), tomatoes, wild mushrooms, or even just a handful of crushed fresh herbs.

Tarallucci - see page 100

Small & Individual

Sometimes small can be beautiful and tasty, too. From mouth-watering appetisers and snacks, such as Yoghurt Cheese and Dukka Filo Tartlets or Tarallucci, to sophisticated individual portions including Avocado and Parmesan Soufflés and Crespelle ai Porri, here is your chance to impress family and guests. Some are very easy to prepare (a few are even designed to get children going in the kitchen); while others, such as the Sublime Onion Tartlets and the Parmigiano Baskets, will take your baking skills up to the next level, making you feel like a real professional.

Crespelle ai Porri

Crespelle, the Italian word for crêpes, are usually smaller than the French kind. Traditionally they are served as a first course, in place of pasta, tied up into little purse-like bundles. If serving them as a main, however, you can simply fold each one into four.

Ingredients

250g/9oz plain flour
500ml/17fl oz milk
4 eggs
50g/2oz butter

FILLING
2 large leeks
50g/2oz butter
50ml/2fl oz white wine (optional)
salt and pepper to taste
100ml/3½fl oz cream

kitchen string to tie up the *crespelle*

Serves 6–8

In a large bowl mix the flour with half of the milk, ensuring you keep the mixture free of lumps. Add the eggs. Keep whisking (best done with an electric beater) until the batter is smooth. Add the rest of the milk and whisk for a few more seconds to incorporate it. Cover the mixture with a plate and let it rest for 1 hour.

Melt the butter in a 20cm (8 inch) non-stick frying pan (no larger or the crêpes will be too large). Remove from the heat and pour the melted butter into the batter. Stir well. (By doing it this way, you will not need to grease the pan between each crêpe.) Return the pan to the heat and pour in about half a ladleful of mixture. Tip the pan a little to allow the batter to spread evenly and cook over a medium heat until the edges of the crêpe start to curl up. Turn it over and cook the other side. A good *crespella* is thin, not too pale, and has a brown mark here and there. Stack the finished crêpes one on top of the other and allow to cool.

To prepare the filling, finely slice the leeks up to the leaves and place in a large frying pan. Add half the butter and place the pan over a medium heat, stirring constantly until the butter is melted. Take care that the leeks do not colour. Add the white wine, if using, reduce heat and cover the pan. Simmer for 10 minutes, stirring occasionally. Season to taste. Stir in the cream and the rest of the butter, then cover and simmer for a further 10 minutes. Remove the lid and cook until all the liquid has evaporated, and the leeks look creamy. Check seasoning and allow to cool.

Place a little filling in the centre of each *crespella* and fold up so that it looks like a little purse. Tie each one with some kitchen string.

Before serving, place the *crespelle* in a steam basket or colander and reheat over boiling water for 5 minutes.

Tips and variations

✱ For a wheat-free version make Buckwheat Crêpes (see opposite).
✱ Choose different fillings to suit the occasion (Italians are particularly fond of the classic spinach and ricotta combination), but remember because they are quite delicate, they are not really suited to spicy flavours. And if you are short on time, don't worry about forming them into little purse shapes, just fold into four.

Buckwheat Crêpes

A traditional dish from Brittany, these versatile French crêpes are a delight to make and eat. They are also wheat- and gluten-free.

Ingredients

50g/2oz butter
200g/7oz buckwheat flour
500ml/17fl oz milk
2 eggs
pinch of salt
1 teaspoon sugar
oil or butter for greasing

Makes 20–25 thin crêpes

Melt the butter in a heatproof jug or bowl placed in a saucepan of boiling water.

Place the flour in a large mixing bowl and slowly stir in half the milk, ensuring there are no lumps. Using an electric beater, mix in the melted butter and the eggs, then slowly pour in the rest of the milk, all the time mixing with the beater. Add the salt and sugar and continue beating until the batter is smooth. Cover with cling film and store in the refrigerator for at least 2 hours.

When you are ready to start cooking the crêpes, grease a non-stick frying pan with just a little oil or butter and heat. Pour half a ladleful of the batter into the hot pan, allowing the batter to run around the pan until the base is covered and the crêpe is very thin. Flip as soon as the underneath is light brown and looks cooked on the bottom, then cook the other side for about 30 seconds to 1 minute. Transfer the cooked crêpe to a plate and cover with a teatowel to keep warm. Repeat this process, greasing the pan between each crêpe or as required, until the batter is finished.

Serve for breakfast, brunch, lunch or dinner, with sweet or savoury fillings.

Tips and variations

✳ For breakfast crêpes, prepare the batter in the evening and leave it in the refrigerator overnight. If you are serving a number of people flip each crêpe as soon as it is ready directly onto individual plates, allowing each person to organise their own fillings.
  If you are not confident about making very thin crêpes, just make them thicker and call them pancakes.
✳ Use half buckwheat and half plain flour for a milder (but not wheat-free) taste.

Pumpkin, Herb and Feta Filo Parcels

The sweet flavour of pumpkin is complemented here by the contrasting sharp feta cheese and the aromatic herbs.

Ingredients

2 tablespoons pumpkin seeds, plus extra
   for sprinkling
1 tablespoon olive oil, plus extra for
   brushing
sprig each of rosemary, sage, thyme
   and marjoram
1 clove garlic, peeled and finely sliced
1kg/2lbs 2oz chopped pumpkin flesh, skin
   and seeds removed
250ml/8fl oz vegetable stock
200g/7oz feta cheese, crumbled
12 sheets filo pastry

Makes 12 parcels

Heat a large frying pan and roast the pumpkin seeds by shaking the pan over the heat until the seeds start popping. Remove from the pan and set aside.

Add the olive oil to the pan. Strip the leaves from the herb sprigs and add to the pan with the garlic. Add the pumpkin flesh and stir for 1 minute, before pouring in the vegetable stock. Cover and simmer until all the liquid has been absorbed and the pumpkin is soft (about 20 minutes). If it takes longer for the stock to evaporate, remove the lid for the last 2–3 minutes. Allow the pumpkin to cool.

Transfer the roasted pumpkin seeds to a mortar and crush them lightly with the pestle. Add the crushed seeds to the cooked pumpkin flesh, then the feta and mix well. Taste to check if any seasoning is required, although this should not be necessary because the stock and the feta are both salty.

Preheat the oven to 180°C (350°F).

Place a sheet of filo pastry sheet on the bench or table so that a short side faces you. Spoon 2 level tablespoons of the mixture on the short side of the pastry nearest you and roll a couple of times, folding in the sides as you go so the edges are sealed and the rolled-up pastry resembles a Chinese spring roll. Repeat this process with the remaining filo sheets and pumpkin mixture. Brush the rolls with olive oil and place on an oven tray lined with baking paper. If desired, sprinkle the top of each roll with the extra pumpkin seeds.

Bake for 25–30 minutes or until the pastry is golden and crunchy.

Serve hot or cold.

Tips and variations

✳ Pumpkin simmered this way with herbs, garlic and vegetable stock is a great vegetable dish to serve alongside a main course. It can also form the base for a delicious pumpkin soup.
✳ For a dairy-free alternative, replace feta with crumbled tofu.
✳ Serve these parcels in summer with a fresh mixed salad, or in winter with roasted root vegetables and gravy.

Porcini Mushroom Vols-au-Vent

Mushroom vols-au-vent are a real blast from the past, but I do love to serve them every now and again, especially for a retro-themed dinner. And nothing beats porcini for an intense mushroom flavour.

Ingredients

15g/½oz dried porcini mushrooms
100ml/3½fl oz water
1 tablespoon plain or high-grade flour
150ml/5½fl oz milk
25g/1oz butter
salt and pepper to taste
2 tablespoons grated edam cheese
  (optional)
12 x 6cm/2½ inch pastry vol-au-vent cases

Serves 4 as a main or 6 as a starter

Break the porcini into small pieces and soak them in the water for 30 minutes.

In a heavy-based saucepan mix the flour with a little of the milk, ensuring there are no lumps. Add the rest of the milk, followed by the porcini and the soaking water, then the butter. Simmer gently, stirring constantly, until the butter is melted and a thick sauce forms. Cook for a more few minutes to soften the mushrooms. Remove from the heat, season to taste and stir in the cheese, if using. (The sauce can be made in advance to this stage and refrigerated.)

Preheat the oven to 180°C (350°F).

Spoon the sauce into the vol-au-vent cases. Place the filled cases on an oven tray lined with baking paper and bake for 15 minutes. Serve immediately.

Tips and variations

✳ For more zing, top the hot pastries with a mixture of chopped garlic and chopped parsley.
✳ Substitute a combination of puréed cauliflower and blue cheese, or spinach and feta, for the mushrooms.

Sublime Onion Tartlets

These tartlets are easy to make, provide a great taste sensation, and look as if they came straight from a very grand restaurant.

Ingredients

2 large onions
50g/2oz butter
4 teaspoons brown sugar
160g/5½oz ready-rolled puff pastry
freshly ground black pepper
4 teaspoons parmesan cheese (optional)

Serves 4

Peel the onions and cut each one in half horizontally. Steam for 5–10 minutes in a steam basket or a colander placed over a saucepan of boiling water until half-cooked (i.e. moist but still firm).

In the meantime melt the butter in a small frying pan over low heat. Add the brown sugar and stir until it forms a lump. Divide the lump into 4 and place each piece in a small tartlet tin or a 9.5cm (3½ inch) ramekin. Place the onions, cut-side down, in the frying pan over medium heat for 2 minutes to absorb the remaining butter, then transfer to the tartlet tins placing one in each tin, cut-side down, on top of the sugar and butter lumps. Pour over any remaining butter from the frying pan.

Preheat the oven to 180°C (350°F).

Divide the puff pastry into 4 equal pieces and use to cover each onion, pressing down with your fingers to create a dome of pastry around the onion top so that a bowler hat shape is formed.

Bake for 20 minutes or until the pastry is golden and perfectly cooked. Remove from the oven and allow to cool for 5 minutes before tipping the pastry cases onto a plate (they should come out very easily).

Serve immediately, covered with freshly ground black pepper and, if desired, grated parmesan cheese.

Tips and variations

* For a more aromatic version add 1 clove to each onion before covering with pastry.
* Sprinkle pastry with a drop of good quality balsamic vinegar instead of parmesan cheese.

Butter Bean Filo Triangles

These lovely filo pastries have a strong Mediterranean flavour and are, literally, full of beans.

Ingredients

½ red onion
1 tablespoon olive oil, plus extra for
   brushing
pinch of paprika
1 x 400g/14oz can butter beans
1 tablespoon tomato paste
salt to taste
2 tablespoons breadcrumbs
few leaves of fresh basil or flat-leaf
   (Italian) parsley or a mixture of both
4 sheets filo pastry

Makes 4 triangles/parcels

Peel and finely chop the onion. Heat a frying pan and sauté the onion in the olive oil. Add the paprika and the beans, including the liquid, and the tomato paste. Cook until the liquid has reduced a little, then add salt to taste. Add the breadcrumbs to the pan, stir in well and remove from the heat. Roughly tear the basil and add to the pan, then set aside.

Preheat the oven to 180°C (350°F).

Place a sheet of filo pastry on the bench or table and spoon a quarter of the bean mixture into a corner. Roll up the pastry to form a triangle, ensuring each side is well enclosed. Repeat this process with the remaining filo and beans. Brush the triangles with olive oil and place on an oven tray lined with baking paper. Bake for 25–30 minutes or until the pastry is golden and crunchy.

Serve hot or cold.

Tips and variations

✳ Use different herbs such as fresh oregano or marjoram or a teaspoon of pesto.

Pastry Cases for Children

More of an idea than a recipe, this can be a fun project for children.

Ingredients

12 x 6cm (2½ inch) ready-baked
   pastry cases
assorted vegetables, e.g. cherry tomatoes,
   carrots, cooked peas, cooked chickpeas
   or beans, baby spinach leaves,
   sautéd leeks, sautéd mushrooms, sautéd
   courgettes (zucchini), sautéd cabbage,
   steamed asparagus, steamed broccoli or
   cauliflower, grilled or roasted capsicums
   (peppers) and eggplant (aubergine)
salt to taste
olive oil and lemon juice for dressing
herbs to decorate (optional)

Makes 12

Cut and cook the vegetables as you wish, or have them raw, just dressed with a little salt, olive oil and lemon juice. Try to have a selection of at least 5 or 6 colours. Make sure the vegetables are cool enough to touch, and let the children fill their own pastry cases (2 or 3 per child) with their favourite vegetables, either one type or a mix. Tell fussy children that they should aim to have more than two colours on their plate. Have fun and make sure to take a photo of all those wonderful creations.

Tips and variations

✳ Vegetables can be sautéed with a little olive oil and salt, possibly a little chopped parsley too. For some vegetables, such as cabbage and broccoli, sauté for a few minutes, then add a little vegetable stock and simmer for a few more minutes. Don't boil the cabbage: it will taste and smell horrible!

Tarallucci

Tarallucci are little ring-shaped snacks from southern Italy and in this version they are boiled like bagels, and then baked. They are great to serve with drinks, and also make a healthy alternative to chips for adults and children.

Ingredients

200g/7oz high-grade flour
pinch of salt
pinch of chilli powder or to taste
4–5 tablespoons olive oil,
  plus a little extra
50ml/2fl oz of water

Makes 50–60

Combine all the ingredients in a large bowl and mix energetically for about 10 minutes until a soft dough is formed. If it is not soft, add another tablespoon of olive oil. Wrap the dough in cling film and leave it to rest for 30 minutes at room temperature.

Take a small piece of dough, leaving the balance still wrapped in the cling film, and roll it into a long, thin grissini-like stick. The high oil content of the dough will probably require you to do a bit of rolling between the palms of your hands as well as on the kitchen bench to avoid it separating. Cut small pieces from the length of pastry and roll them around the tip of your finger, pinching the ends together to form a little ring. Set aside and continue working until all the wrapped dough has been used. (The size of *tarallucci* varies from bakery to bakery. I like to make small ones, but there are some that look more like bangles than little rings! It is up to you.)

Bring a large saucepan of water to the boil and drop in the *tarallucci*, a few at the time, and cook for about 2–3 minutes until they rise to the surface. Using a slotted spoon, remove them from the pan and transfer to a teatowel to dry.

Preheat the oven to 180°C (350°F).

Grease an oven tray with the extra olive oil (you only need a little). Position as many *tarallucci* as will comfortably fit on the tray and bake for 10 minutes. Remove from the oven and turn each piece over before baking for a further 10 minutes. Allow to cool completely before serving or store in an airtight container for up to 1 month.

Tips and variations

* Make them with a friend – it takes about a third of the time!
* Substitute a few fennel seeds for the chilli.
* Easy *tarallucci* can be made by using the recipe for Focaccia with Olives dough (see page 39) with the addition of a pinch of chilli – simply bake until golden, thus skipping the boiling stage.

Yoghurt Cheese and Dukka Filo Tartlets

While easy to make, the *labneh* (yoghurt cheese) filling for these tartlets requires time and planning, so I suggest using ready-made filo tartlets to compensate. And when you serve them, be prepared for lots of compliments.

Ingredients

LABNEH
500g/1lb 2oz Greek-style yoghurt
200ml/7fl oz olive oil
½ teaspoon salt
½ tablespoon dried oregano

DUKKA
2 tablespoons unpeeled almonds
1 tablespoon sesame seeds
  (use a mixture of black and white seeds)
1 tablespoon pumpkin seeds
1 teaspoon cumin seeds
1 teaspoon rock salt
pinch of paprika

30 ready-made filo party tartlets
30 baby spinach leaves
10–12 small cherry tomatoes or
  tiny fresh herb sprigs for decorating

Makes 30 tartlets

To make the *labneh*, line a large sieve with a piece of muslin or cheesecloth, allowing some overhang. Fill with the yoghurt and fold the cloth over to cover. Place the sieve over a bowl and gently press the yoghurt to extract some liquid. Transfer to the refrigerator and store for 2 days, pressing the yoghurt gently from time to time to encourage the liquid to seep into the bowl. (You will need to drain the liquid from the bowl from time to time.) After 2 days the yoghurt should be quite hard. Oil your hands and shape the yoghurt into 30 small balls. As you make them, place them one at a time in a large glass or ceramic jar filled with the olive oil, salt and oregano. Top with more oil if required and store for up to 4 weeks.

To make the dukka, place the almonds in a baking dish or pan and roast in a hot 180°C (350°F) oven for 3–4 minutes. Add the rest of the seeds and roast for a further 3 minutes, shaking the pan a couple of times to ensure they don't stick and burn. Allow to cool completely, then transfer to a food processor. Add the salt and paprika and pulse until the nuts and seeds are reduced to very fine crumbs. Store in a sealed container for up to 2 weeks.

To assemble, place a baby spinach leaf in the base of each filo tartlet. Spread the dukka out on a large tray. Drain the *labneh* balls (keep the oil for making dips or dressings) and roll in the dukka. Place each ball as it is rolled in a tartlet and top with a slice of cherry tomato or herb sprig. Serve within a few hours.

Tips and variations

✳ Use a mini muffin tray to make your own filo tartlets. Simply turn the tray upside down and spray with oil. Cut about 4 sheets of filo into 5cm (2 inch) rounds and place over the oiled moulds. Spray with more oil and bake, tray and all, in a preheated 180°C (350°F) oven for a few minutes until they start to turn golden brown around the edges. Remove from the oven and allow to cool completely before removing from their moulds.

Focaccia Crispy Sticks

This is a good way of using leftover stale focaccia. The resulting sticks are perfect for soups, dips, an antipasto platter or even by themselves with a glass of dry white wine.

Ingredients

1 x quantity stale focaccia
olive oil spray

Preheat the oven to 180°C (350°F).

Cut the bread lengthways into 1cm (⅓ inch) thick slices so you end up with long pieces. Place the bread on a baking tray lined with baking paper and spray each piece with olive oil. Bake for a few minutes until the sticks start to colour and curl up. Turn each piece over and bake on the other side. Allow to cool, then store in an airtight container.

Tips and variations

* Make Italian *crostini* (crispbread) the same way using any leftover bread. My mother-in-law uses thin slices of stale baguette, which are delicious!

Puff Pastry Cheese and Spice Fans

I make these little pastry treats with my children when they feel like baking. Ready-rolled puff pastry is fine, but of course they will taste even better if you make your own (see page 54).

Ingredients

2 tablespoons grated edam cheese
pinch of paprika
pinch of cumin seeds
pinch of salt
1 x 160g/5½oz sheet ready-rolled
   puff pastry

Makes 8 fans

Preheat the oven to 180°C (350°F).

Spread the grated cheese, paprika, cumin seeds and salt over the sheet of pastry. Roll the two sides of the pastry sheet towards each other so they meet in the centre. Cut into 16 pieces (it is easier to do this starting from the centre). Take 2 of the heart-shaped pieces at a time and using your fingers, press them together at the base to form a fan shape.

Place the fans on a baking tray lined with baking paper and bake for 15 minutes. Serve hot or cold.

Tips and variations

✳ Replace spices with dried herbs such as oregano or sage. For a sweet version, omit the filling, then sprinkle generously with caster sugar. A real Italian treat!

Avocado and Parmesan Soufflés

These easy and wheat-free soufflés don't have a strong 'eggy' taste and can be made in a few minutes – perfect to serve as an entrée or for a sophisticated late supper.

Ingredients

1 ripe avocado
few drops of lemon juice
pinch of salt
2 teaspoons grated parmesan cheese
4 tablespoons cream
2 eggs, separated
butter for greasing

Serves 3

Peel the avocado, then mash in a bowl with the lemon juice. Add the salt, parmesan, cream and the egg yolks.

In a separate bowl whip the egg whites into very stiff peaks, ideally using an electric beater, and set aside briefly. Transfer the unrinsed beater to the avocado mixture and gently beat until soft and airy.

Preheat the oven to 200°C (400°F).

Grease 3 small soufflé ramekins with butter. Gently fold the beaten egg whites into the avocado mixture, ensuring that the mixture stays soft and airy. Spoon into the ramekins, gently levelling the top of each with the back of the spoon.

Bake for 10–15 minutes or until lightly coloured on top. (Do not overcook, and avoid opening the oven door while they are baking or they will deflate.)

Serve immediately.

Tips and variations

✳ If you want to intensify the lovely light green colour of these soufflés, just add a sprinkle of powdered barley grass (available from health food stores) to the avocado mixture.

Parmigiano Baskets

These little baskets of grated Parmigiano Reggiano add a professional touch and they work well as a substantial starter or as a light main. Use real Italian parmesan cheese, either Parmigiano Reggiano or Grana Padano, for the baskets because local parmesan-style cheese will not work.

Ingredients

8 heaped tablespoons grated Parmigiano Reggiano, plus a little extra

FILLING
½ cauliflower
1 medium carrot
12 fresh asparagus spears
1 teaspoon balsamic vinegar
½ teaspoon salt
1 tablespoon extra virgin olive oil
4 hard-boiled eggs (best if the yolks are still a little soft)

Serves 4

Preheat the oven to 180°C (350°F).

Line an oven tray with a sheet of baking paper. Sprinkle 2 tablespoons of the cheese in a circle about the size of a CD on the middle of the baking paper. Bake for 1 minute or until the cheese starts bubbling, then remove the tray from the oven. Lift the baking paper, with the melted cheese attached, and place it over an inverted glass. Gently peel off the baking paper so that the soft cheese takes the shape of a basket. Allow to cool completely. Repeat with the remaining cheese until you have 4 baskets.

Chop the cauliflower into fork-sized pieces. Boil or steam until tender, but still a little crunchy. Place the cooked cauliflower in a bowl filled with cold water to keep it crisp. Prepare the carrot and asparagus and cook, again either boiling or steaming, until just crunchy, but in separate pans so they do not take on the same taste. Place in the cold water until ready to serve.

Drain the vegetables. Cut each asparagus piece into 3 and transfer to a salad bowl. Add the other vegetables. Blend the balsamic vinegar with the salt in a large serving spoon and add the olive oil. Toss the mixture through the vegetables, mixing well.

Fill the parmesan baskets with the dressed vegetables. Shell the eggs, cut in half lengthways and place a half in each basket. Serve immediately.

Tips and variations

✳ For a dairy-free alternative, make baskets using ready-made filo party tartlets (see page 101).
✳ Replace the asparagus with steamed broccoli or snow peas and contrast with potatoes or turnips, and cherry tomatoes or beetroot. Save the water from boiling the vegetables to make stock.

Parmesan and Basil Frittata - see page 116

Frittata & Omelettes

It has often been said that if you have an egg at hand, then you have a meal. And what could be easier to whip up than a quick frittata!

In this chapter you will find many frittata variations so that your eggs will go an impressively long way, as well as recipes for savoury tarts that don't have a pastry base or shell. From a rustic Tortilla Española through to a sophisticated Nasturtium Clafoutis, I guarantee these recipes, which I have made hundreds of times, will convert even the most dedicated consumers of take-away meals.

Asparagus Omelette with Camembert

A very simple yet sophisticated omelette that can be whipped up in just a few minutes. Although this recipe is for one individual omelette, you can, of course, double the ingredients.

Ingredients

5–6 fresh asparagus spears
1 teaspoon olive oil
1 egg
salt and pepper to taste
1 tablespoon water
1 slice camembert cheese

Serves 1

Wash the asparagus and cut off the hard end of the stalk. Steam for just a few minutes, depending on thickness, until just cooked and still bright green.

While the asparagus are cooking gently heat a small frying pan greased with the olive oil. Break the egg into a bowl, add a little salt and pepper and the water and mix with a fork. Pour the egg mixture into the pan and allow it to spread around the pan. Quickly drain the asparagus and place over half of the omelette. Top with the camembert and fold the omelette over to enclose the filling and make a half-moon shape. Cook the omelette for a further 30 seconds, then turn to cook the other side. Slide onto a plate and enjoy immediately.

Tips and variations

✳ If cooking for more than one, have another larger frying pan at hand: keep it warm and as soon as you fold the first omelette, place it in the bigger pan to keep warm while you make the next one.
✳ For a change, substitute broccolini, long green beans or spinach for the asparagus.

Easy Baked Frittata

This is probably one of the easiest and most convenient frittata recipes. It uses just a few ingredients and no flipping is required!

Ingredients

5 spring onions
6 eggs
100ml/3½fl oz cream
generous pinch of salt
½ teaspoon paprika
small handful of rocket leaves
2 tablespoons olive oil
4–5 vine-ripened tomatoes (optional)

Serves 4 as a main course

Preheat the oven to 180°C (350°F).

Finely chop 1 spring onion and set the rest aside. In a mixing bowl whisk the eggs with the cream, salt and paprika. Add the chopped spring onion and the rocket leaves.

Grease a 20cm (8 inch) round or square baking dish or line it with baking paper, add the oil and heat in the oven for 2–3 minutes until the oil is hot. Remove the baking dish from the oven and pour in the frittata mixture. Arrange the reserved whole spring onions on top and the tomatoes, if using. Cover with a sheet of aluminium foil and bake for 20 minutes. Turn off heat, remove the foil, and leave the frittata in the still-warm oven for 10 minutes or until the eggs are set.

Serve hot or cold.

Tips and variations

* Sprinkle a little grated cheese on top after removing the foil.
* Add more vegetables to the egg mixture, e.g. steamed asparagus, green beans, cherry tomatoes, spinach – anything that takes your fancy.

Silverbeet Frittata

My friend Sandra makes the best silverbeet frittata ever! Here is my version of her delicious dish.

Ingredients

250g/9oz silverbeet
pinch of salt
4 eggs
salt, pepper and freshly ground nutmeg
   to taste
1 tablespoon grated parmesan cheese
oil for cooking

Serves 4

Wash the silverbeet. Cut off the white stalks and chop into small pieces. Place the chopped stalks in a large saucepan and simmer (with no added water) for 2–3 minutes. In the meantime chop the green leaves and add them to the pan along with a pinch of salt. Simmer for a few more minutes until completely wilted.

In a bowl whisk the eggs with the seasonings and parmesan. Add the silverbeet.

Oil a frying pan and heat. When the pan is hot, pour in the frittata mixture. Cover and cook on low until golden underneath. Flip the frittata (best done by flipping it out of the pan, onto the frying pan lid and then sliding it back in the pan) and cook the other side.

Tips and variations

* Use spinach or kale instead of silverbeet.
* Allow to cool completely, then cut into small cubes and toss in a fancy green salad.

Frittata di Spaghetti

Make this frittata when you have leftover cooked spaghetti or other kinds of pasta.

Ingredients

4 eggs
salt, pepper and nutmeg to taste
1 tablespoon chopped Italian
   (flat-leaf) parsley
400g/14oz cooked spaghetti
olive oil for cooking

Serves 4

In a bowl whisk the eggs with the salt, pepper, nutmeg and parsley. Chop the pasta into manageable pieces and stir into the egg mixture. Lightly oil a frying pan and heat. Add the frittata mixture, cover and cook on low until golden underneath. Flip the frittata (best done by flipping it out of the pan, onto the frying pan lid and then sliding it back in the pan) and cook the other side.

Tips and variations

* Any type of leftover spaghetti works well in this frittata, especially those made with a tomato or pesto sauce, but the quantity is important so do ensure you weigh it first.

Frittatone

Frittatone is my name for this dish because it is a big frittata full of many different goodies – perfect for a Sunday brunch or an informal dinner. In spring I like to use asparagus, otherwise green beans will do fine.

Ingredients

2 tablespoons olive oil

pinch of salt

1 each red, yellow and green capsicums
 (peppers), deseeded and
 chopped into strips

2 tablespoons pitted black olives

1 bunch of asparagus or
 handful of green beans

6 eggs

200ml/7fl oz single or double cream

salt, pepper and freshly grated
 nutmeg to taste

1 whole mozzarella cheese, diced

small handful of fresh basil leaves,
 roughly torn

sprig of cherry vine-ripened tomatoes
 on the vine

Serves 6–8

Heat the olive oil and the salt in a frying pan. Sauté the chopped capsicums for 5 minutes, then turn off the heat and cover. Allow the capsicums to cool in the pan before removing the skin (the steam produced by covering them should allow the skins to be easily removed.) Return the capsicums to the pan, add the olives and stir, then set aside. The recipe can be prepared to this point 1 day ahead and is actually better done in advance because the olives will absorb more flavour from the capsicums and olive oil.

Wash the asparagus and cut off the hard end of the stalk. Steam for just a few minutes, depending on their thickness, until just cooked and still bright green. Chop as desired.

Preheat the oven to 180°C (350°F).

In a large bowl whisk the eggs and cream with an electric beater. Season to taste. Fold in the capsicum mixture, then the asparagus, followed by the mozzarella and the basil. Pour the mixture into a rectangular lasagne dish lined with baking paper. Position the sprig of cherry tomatoes on top, pushing them gently into the frittata mixture so they are half absorbed.

Bake for 20–30 minutes (frittata is cooked when a toothpick inserted into the centre comes out clean).

Serve hot or cold.

Tips and variations

✳ For a sharper taste, substitute feta cheese in place of the mozzarella.

✳ Use as many favourite or seasonal vegetables as you want – no flipping is required so you can overload it as much as you like.

✳ If the frittata browns too quickly on top but is still liquid in the centre, cover with a sheet of aluminium foil halfway through baking.

Green Bean Frittata

A very easy baked frittata that looks as good as it tastes.

Ingredients

400g/14oz green beans
1 clove garlic, peeled and sliced
1 tablespoon olive oil
200ml/7fl oz water
1 teaspoon tomato paste
pinch of dried oregano
salt to taste
4 eggs
pinch of salt
freshly ground black pepper
freshly ground nutmeg
4 cherry tomatoes (optional)

Serves 3–4

Wash and trim the beans. Place in a frying pan with the garlic and olive oil and sauté for 2–3 minutes. Add the water, tomato paste, oregano and salt. Cover and simmer for 15–20 minutes until all the water has been absorbed.

In a mixing bowl lightly whisk the eggs with the salt, pepper and nutmeg.

Preheat the oven to 180°C (350°F).

Line a 20cm (8 inch) baking dish with baking paper and arrange the green beans on the base. Add the cherry tomatoes, if using, so that there will be one per slice. Pour in the egg mixture and bake for 20 minutes or until the frittata looks golden and fragrant. Remove from the oven and invert onto a serving plate. Remove the baking paper and serve hot or cold, accompanied by potatoes (which go well with green beans) or a green salad.

Tips and variations

* Substitute lightly steamed asparagus or broccoli for the green beans.
* Use 1 teaspoon of pesto instead of tomato paste.
* Add some grated cheese to the egg mixture for a richer frittata.

Torta di Riso

This is a tasty and easy tart, but it's made without a crust so that it is similar to a French tian. To save time I use a bought pack of ready-washed baby spinach leaves, but leaves from your veggie garden will taste even better.

Ingredients

150g/5½oz long grain rice
120g/4oz ready-washed baby
  spinach leaves
3 eggs
100ml/3½fl oz cream
salt, pepper and freshly ground nutmeg
  to taste
grated edam-style cheese (optional)

Serves 4 as a main or 6–8 as an entrée

Boil the rice in plenty of salted water for 10 minutes.

Place the spinach leaves in a large bowl. Drain the rice and add to the spinach, stirring, until the leaves start to wilt from the heat.

Preheat the oven to 180°C (350°F).

In a separate bowl mix the eggs with the cream and the seasonings. Fold the egg mixture into the rice and pour into a 20cm (8 inch) round baking dish (either terracotta, in which case it should be lightly oiled, or a metal dish lined with baking paper). If desired, sprinkle a little grated cheese on the top, then bake for 30 minutes.

Serve hot or cold, accompanied by a tomato and green salad.

Tips and variations

✳ Although long grain rice works better for this dish, short grain rice will do.
✳ Young silverbeet, kale and other greens can be used instead of spinach.

Torta di Patate

While everybody in my family makes this *torta*, Mamma seems to have a special touch – hers has a lovely crunchy crust and it never breaks.

Ingredients

500g/1lb 1oz roasted or baked potatoes, cooled
1 tablespoon chopped Italian (flat-leaf) parsley
1 clove garlic, peeled and crushed
salt, pepper and freshly ground nutmeg to taste
3–4 tablespoons olive oil

Serves 3–4

In a large bowl mash the potatoes. Add the parsley, garlic and seasonings and mix well. Form the mixture into a 2.5cm (1 inch) thick disc, slightly smaller than the frying pan in which it will be cooked. Make it as compact as possible by patting it down with a wooden spoon or with your hands.

Preheat the oven to 180°C (350°F).

Heat the oil in a frying pan. When the pan is hot, place the potato cake inside and gently fry, allowing the cake to move around the pan without sticking or losing its shape until golden underneath. Flip the *torta*, taking care in the process because the cake will still be very soft (best done by flipping it out of the pan, onto the frying pan lid, and then sliding it back in the pan). You may need to add a little extra oil before sliding it back in and cooking the other side. Transfer the *torta* to the oven (if your pan is not ovenproof, tip out the *torta* onto an oven tray) and bake for 15–20 minutes until the crust is crunchy and the inside so soft that it can be cut with a fork. Eat immediately.

Tips and variations

* Add 1 egg and some grated parmesan cheese to the potato mixture for a richer taste and to help the mixture stick together.

Frittata alla Mentuccia

Mentuccia, a wild mint my dad picks in his village in the Apennines of the Emilia Romagna region, goes well with eggs. Fortunately, for those of us outside Italy, other kinds of garden mint can easily be substituted.

Ingredients

6 eggs
2 tablespoons grated pecorino cheese
salt to taste
small handful of fresh mint leaves, roughly torn plus extra for decoration (optional)
oil for cooking

Serves 4

In a bowl whisk the eggs with a fork. Add the cheese, salt and the mint leaves.

Lightly oil a medium frying pan and heat. Add the frittata mixture, cover and cook on low until golden underneath. Flip the frittata (best done by flipping it out of the pan, onto the frying pan lid and then sliding it back in the pan) and cook the other side. Turn out onto a serving plate and enjoy, hot or cold, decorated with mint as desired.

Tips and variations

* Other herbs can be substituted, e.g. thyme, marjoram or any herb you prefer.

Onion and Courgette Frittata

Although onion frittata is one of the most basic and popular Italian egg dishes, I like to add courgettes (zucchini), which are very easy to digest and add a bit of colour.

Ingredients

1 onion
4 courgettes (zucchini)
1 tablespoon olive oil
pinch of salt
4 eggs
extra salt and pepper to taste
freshly ground nutmeg (optional)
small handful of fresh basil leaves,
    roughly torn
oil for cooking

Serves 4

Peel and finely chop the onion and slice the courgettes. Place in a frying pan with the olive oil and the salt over medium heat. Sauté for 1 minute, then cover and simmer on low for 8–10 minutes until the vegetables are well cooked, but not mushy. Uncover and simmer for a few more minutes until all the water has evaporated.

In the meantime, lightly whisk the eggs with a little salt and pepper, and the nutmeg if using. Add the basil and the courgette mixture. Generously oil a clean frying pan and heat. When the pan is hot, add the frittata mixture. Cover and cook on low until golden underneath. Flip the frittata (best done by flipping it out of the pan, onto the frying pan lid and then sliding it back in the pan) and cook on the other side. Enjoy hot or eat cold.

Tips and variations

✳ Instead of cooking them first, grate the courgettes and add to the egg mixture.
✳ Substitute a few courgette petals for the basil.

Tortilla Española

In my student days in London I used to spend a lot of time with Spanish friends. They regularly made tortilla because it was cheap and easy student food. I still recall being told off when I asked if it was a frittata!

Ingredients

2 medium to large potatoes, peeled
1 small onion, peeled
3 tablespoons olive oil
salt to taste
4 eggs
extra salt (optional)

Serves 4 as a main (or slice and
    serve as tapas)

Finely slice or cube the potatoes and pat dry with a teatowel. Finely slice the onion.

Heat 2 tablespoons of the oil in a frying pan. When the pan is hot, add the salt, then sauté the potato and onion slices for about 10 minutes until almost cooked but still white and translucent, stirring often to ensure they do not burn.

In a mixing bowl lightly whisk the eggs using a fork and the extra salt if desired. Add the cooked potato and onion to the egg mixture and fold it in. Set aside to stand for 10–15 minutes.

Heat the remaining oil in the frying pan. When the pan is hot, add the tortilla mixture and cook over low heat. Flip the tortilla (best done by flipping it out of the pan, onto the frying pan lid, and then sliding it back in the pan) and cook the other side.

Serve hot or cold.

Tips and variations

✳ Mash the potatoes a little before putting them in the egg mixture
✳ If the eggs take too long to set, cover the frying pan with a lid during cooking.

Rolled Omelette with Nori and Sesame Seeds

The perfect Japanese omelette takes time to master. It helps if you have a square frying pan and a quick hand. However, here is a simplified version, using a conventional (round) frying pan that still produces professional results.

Ingredients

4 eggs
100ml/3½fl oz water
1 tablespoon Japanese soy sauce
1 sheet nori (seaweed)
oil for cooking
1 tablespoon toasted sesame seeds

Serves 2 as a main or 4 as a starter

Lightly mix the eggs with the water and soy sauce using a fork or chopsticks.

Heat a small 13cm (5 inch) non-stick oiled frying pan. When the pan is hot, pour in the egg mixture. Reduce heat to low and cover. Cook for 2 minutes, then lift the omelette around the sides to allow some of the uncooked egg mixture to run underneath. Repeat every 2 minutes until it no longer runs but the top is still a bit sticky. Place the nori on top, then flip the omelette, nori-side up, onto a sushi rolling mat.

Roll up the omelette so that from side-on the nori can be seen to form a spiral pattern, then allow to cool, still rolled in the mat. At this stage the hot egg mixture is still cooking and will set into the desired shape – a perfect tube, or square, or triangle – depending on your rolling skills.

Spread the sesame seeds over a sheet of cling film. When the omelette is completely cool, roll it in the seeds, then wrap it in the cling film twisting the film at each end so that it resembles a giant paper-wrapped toffee.

Store in the fridge until ready to serve, at which time it should be cut into slices and accompanied by grated daikon or radish.

Tips and variations

✳ A traditional Japanese omelette will usually contain a light fish or seaweed stock rather than water (which, in certain parts of Japan including Tokyo, is sweetened by adding 1 teaspoon of sugar).
✳ Little square frying pans can be found in Asian or specialised kitchen shops.

Glossary

BUCKWHEAT: A native of Central Asia and related to the rhubarb family, buckwheat produces nutrient-rich flour suitable for wheat-intolerant people and is used mainly for making crêpes, blinis and Japanese soba noodles.

DAIKON: A turnip-shaped Oriental radish readily available from Asian food and vegetable shops and markets. It is usually used raw, but can also be pickled.

DUKKA: A spice and nut mixture of Egyptian origins that can be sprinkled on food or used as a dip.

FENNEL: This popular Italian vegetable has a light aniseed taste; the bulbs can be eaten either raw or cooked and the seeds, which are rich in essential oils, can be used to make teas and herbal medicines, as well as flavouring food and liqueurs.

LABNEH: A yoghurt cheese originating in the Middle East, also known as *labna*, *lebney*, *gibne* and *labaneh*.

MOZZARELLA: White in colour, semi-soft and moist, this Italian cheese can be made from buffalo's milk (*mozzarella di bufala*) or cow's milk (*fiordilatte*).

PECORINO: The most famous types of this Italian sheep's milk cheese are pecorino romano and pecorino sardo, from Rome and Sardinia respectively. Hard pecorino can be grated just like parmesan cheese.

PORCINI: These Italian mushrooms (*Boletus edulis*) can be eaten fresh or, outside of Italy, purchased dried from delicatessen shops and good supermarkets. Dried mushrooms should be soaked before using.

RICOTTA: Italian curd cheese that can be eaten uncooked but more usually used in a number of savoury and sweet dishes.

SCAMORZA: Cow's cheese made in a similar way to mozzarella, then tied with a string and hung to mature or, in the case of *scamorza affumicata*, smoked.

SPELT: From the wheat family, but with a different genetic structure, spelt produces flour that is often better tolerated by those who are allergic to common wheat products.

Conversion Tables

The following amounts have been rounded up or down for convenience. All have been kitchen tested.

METRIC TO IMPERIAL

10-15g	½oz
20g	¾oz
30g	1oz
40g	1½oz
50-60g	2oz
75-85g	3oz
100g	3½oz
125g	4oz
150g	5oz
175g	6oz
200g	7oz
225g	8oz
250g	9oz
300g	10½oz
350g	12oz
400g	14oz
450g	1lb
500g	1lb 2oz
600g	1lb 5oz
750g	1lb 10oz
1kg	2lb 3oz

50-55ml	2fl oz
75ml	3fl oz
100ml	3½fl oz
120ml	4fl oz
150ml	5fl oz
170ml	6fl oz
200ml	7fl oz
225ml	8fl oz
250ml	8½fl oz
300ml	10fl oz
400ml	13fl oz
500ml	17fl oz
600ml	20fl oz
750ml	25fl oz
1 litre	34fl oz

Please note:
1 pint in the UK = 16fl oz
1 pint in the USA = 20fl oz

OVEN TEMPERATURES

Celsius	Fahrenheit	Gas Mark
120°	250°	1
150°	300°	2
160°	325°	3
180°	350°	4
190°	375°	5
200°	400°	6
220°	425°	7

BAKING TIN SIZES

Common square and rectangular baking pan sizes:

20x20cm	8x8 inch
23x23cm	9x9 inch
23x13cm	9x5 inch loaf pan/tin

Common round baking pan sizes:

20cm	8 inch
23cm	9 inch
25cm	10 inch

Note baking paper = non-stick baking parchment.

TABLESPOON MEASURES

In New Zealand, South Africa, the UK and the USA 1 tablespoon equals 15ml. In Australia 1 tablespoon equals 20ml.

Capsicum and Mozzarella Pie - see page 62

Index

These symbols indicate: ○ Dairy-free recipe □ Wheat-free recipe

Clockwise from top left: Onion and Courgette Frittata - see page 119; Erbazzone - see page 65; Torta Rustica - see page 87; Delicatessen Pie - see page 61.

Acknowledgements

A big thank you to my family and friends who enthusiastically tasted all my recipes, and in particular to my husband, Peter, and my children, Arantxa and Max. Thanks to all the staff at New Holland Publishers NZ, to project manager Renée Lang, designer Rachel Kirkland and last but not least, photographer Shaun Cato-Symonds.

Finally, thanks to my graceful models listed here in alphabetical order:
Amylie, Brigitte, David, Diana, Jonathan and Max.

Tableware: Small Acorns, Freedom Furniture and the author's private collection
Wine: Cracroft Chase Vineyard Pinot Gris. Beer: DB Breweries (Monteiths)